What Women Want
And How to Give it to Them
By Lauren Atterbery

WHAT WOMEN WANT

And How to Give It to Them

What Women Want ... And How to Give it to Them

Editors: Donna Melillo, April Miller
Cover Design: Jason Kauffmann / Firelight Interactive / firelightinteractive.com
Interior Design: Rick Soldin / book-comp.com

Indigo River Publishing
3 West Garden Street Ste. 352
Pensacola, FL 32502
www.indigoriverpublishing.com

Ordering Information:
Quantity sales: Special discounts are available on quantity purchases by corporations, associations, and others. For details, contact the publisher at the address above.

Orders by U.S. trade bookstores and wholesalers: Please contact the publisher at the address above.

Printed in the United States of America

Library of Congress Control Number: 2013958055

ISBN: 978-0-9860493-2-3

First Edition

*With Indigo River Publishing, you can always expect great books, strong voices, and meaningful messages.
Most importantly, you'll always find ... words worth reading.*

I would like to dedicate this book to Jon, Nate, Shaun, and Darric for being my go-to guys—there for me without question. I would also like to dedicate it to my son Luca, who will be perpetually embarrassed by this as he grows up. I love you guys!

Darric—
Thank you for all of your support through all of this. ☺
I love you.
— Lauren Atterbery

Contents

Prologue

Don't Let Her Catch You Reading This Book

Whether you are a single, dating, or married man, I'm willing to bet you've had your share of frustrations or complications with your occasional girlfriend, lover, or wife. There may have been times you wished that there was some sort of female secret decoder ring in the bottom of your Cracker Jack box, or at the very least, you had a mute button. (Probably the latter if you're already married.) Fellas, although a female translator or manual would be worth all the gold in Fort Knox and lifetime no-limit fishing, they, much like unicorns and Santa Claus, just don't exist.

How can you make her want you or turn the odds in your favor when she gets that look in her eye that says, "You'll pay for this in blood, sweat, and credit card bills?"

Let me teach you. What qualifies me? I'm a woman. And I'm friends with lots of women, and women love to talk. I have listened to friends complain over the years about the things that men have done and what

they wish they had done instead. I know the actions, reactions, and solutions that women are looking for in every situation. Trust me—I've been there before. I'm not saying my relationships have been perfect. (I've been divorced, so I learned from my successes and failures—this only adds to my expertise.) I'm going to let you in on those solutions so that ultimately, you can be the hero in every situation.

The first piece of advice I have to offer is this: don't *ever* let her catch you reading this book. Trust me; women don't want to see that you are working on yourself. They want the illusion that you have too much confidence to hang out in the self-help section of your local Barnes & Noble. She sees that and she thinks, "Obviously he has issues. If he can't even take care of his own issues, how can he take care of me?" Deep down, women want to know that they are going to be taken care of and that you are the type of man who can fix the plumbing and your own emotional issues without a self-help book. Although that girl you're friends with and secretly hope to date will tell you, "I think it's great to see a guy working on himself," chances are she isn't going to accept any dates with that guy.

With that said, keep reading self-help books. Women can be a bit shallow at times without meaning to, and self-help books help you figure out who you are and what you want. Just don't advertise you're doing it if you want her to think you're a big, burly, confident man like the guy on the paper towel roll.

No matter what the situation, you have to make the woman work for your attention just a little bit. Have you ever heard the saying, "You get out what you put in?" Women need to feel like it wasn't easy as pie to get you. If it was too easy, then why was it so easy? What's wrong with you? Most likely nothing. Men and women just think differently. That's why this book will help. Men don't understand women, so I am here to help you know what women actually want ... and how to give it to them.

So You Want a Date

Maybe you're not ready to settle down into a committed relationship; you just want to enjoy the single life for a while. But you still want to be able to attract women and get to know them. Stop listening to your other male friends—they don't know how to do it either. Old, tired pickup lines, outrageous statements, poor choices of clothing, and the worst— poor hygiene—make you stand out ... and not in a good way. It all starts with confidence and proper preparation. You have one chance to make a good impression, so make it count! So how *do* you attract women? Buckle your seatbelt; I'm about to tell you the secret.

Women want a confident man. Notice I said confident, *not* cocky. Confidence can only be faked to an extent. However, everyone is good at *something*. Find whatever it is that you are good at and remind yourself of it whenever you are feeling insecure. For example, when you see a woman who looks like she just walked straight off the runway, and you start to think, "Why would she be with a guy like me?"

remember that other people look at you with respect because you are the smartest or hardest-working guy they know. Maybe you're the best underpaid computer programmer on the block, or you're a teacher who is amazing with children. Remind yourself of how really good you are at said thing, and that confidence will shine through. When it comes from something real, it will be less likely to be mistaken for arrogance.

At this point in your life, if you can't think of anything you are amazing at, get off your lazy tookus and get a hobby. Do it until you are good at it, and then continue reading this book.

Once you've got some confidence built up, the next thing you need to work on is your image. If you are rolling up to the bar or concert in your favorite all-white tennis shoes, jean shorts, and braided belt, you might as well just stay home. Get up and look at yourself in the mirror—now! You can work with whatever you have, but just realize that some things don't happen overnight.

If you're fat, join the gym and do cardio until you lose some of the excess pounds. Girls don't mind a big teddy bear, but teddy bears are cuddly, not sexy. So if that is your approach, quick pick-ups are out. If you are willing to commit to working on yourself, it's still okay to be bigger, but get some muscles in there. Think Vin Diesel in Triple X, not Chris Farley in SNL.

Next, take a look at your hair. If you are going bald, don't sweat it—shave it. Bald heads can be sexy, but fully commit. If you've got a good head of hair, that's great. Being single should be reckless and messy, like your hair. Don't have it perfectly parted and hair sprayed; let it be touchable. Girls will want to run their fingers through it. To achieve this look, wash it, dry it, and put some product in it. Product you say? If you are wondering what the heck that is, you're normal. Go in the hair care aisle of Wal-Mart and grab some kind of cream for wavy hair. Do not—I repeat—do not buy gel. Buy a *cream*; put a quarter-sized dollop in your dry hair, and go. It's as easy as that, you lucky bastard.

Two days of stubble on your face is good too. The more you look like a tortured artist, the better off you are. Clean-shaven is for boyfriends. However, unless you are an orthodox Jew, don't grow a beard; and goatees that are braidable are disgusting. Now look at your eyebrows. Unibrows are gross, so pluck it or get it waxed, Groucho Marx. Only Hugh Atchison can pull off that look.

Then look at your clothes. You are going to need to project what women find sexy, and every woman wants a "bad boy." Dangerous is your new mantra. Dangerous men don't do things like tuck in their shirts, and they don't wear tennis shoes anywhere but the

gym. I am going to give you a rundown of some things you could wear, but here is an easier piece of advice: Even though you might feel uncomfortable doing this, go to the magazine section of any book or department store and grab a woman's magazine like *Vogue* or *Cosmopolitan*. These magazines are designed to tell women what they want and what they should expect. You might benefit from reading the articles, but that depends on who you're trying to date.

Flip through the advertisements and take a look at what the men are wearing. Whether they know it or not, women subconsciously see these and decide that those are the kind of men they find attractive. So study their hair and their clothes and find an outfit you can live with.

I can tell you that a woman knows within the first ten seconds of seeing a guy whether or not she is interested. If she sees you wearing gym shoes or your favorite Family Guy t-shirt, she's not going to give you the time of day.

Your outfit should include dark-wash jeans and boots or non-lace-up shoes. When I say boots, I mean motorcycle, not cowboy or hiking. If you are confident enough, you can wear light jeans that have holes in them—but do so carefully and only if your legs are great.

You should wear a t-shirt (not the kind you got donating blood) and a jacket of some sort, preferably a nice leather one. Forgo jewelry of any kind with the exception of rings that are silver. If said ring is on your left ring finger, stop being a jerk and go back to your wife. An outfit like this, along with your touchable hair, is the way to catch a girl's attention.

Don't think you can afford an outfit like this? Remember, this is an investment. However, you should never have to pay full price for this stuff. Now I know this is probably boring for you to read about, but I'll let you in on a favorite secret of most women: discount designer stores. Marshall's, T.J. Maxx, and DSW Shoes are all places where you can get these clothes and shoes for less than a quarter of the original price. Target can usually be counted on for plaid, rugged-man shirts in the winter too. You will spend less there on one outfit than you will on your bar tab, and you will spend less money on your bar tab if you leave early with the girl of your dreams.

Also, they sell boxer briefs and socks there. Please don't ruin your carefully planned image by wearing white socks or tightie-whities. Wear dark-colored boxer briefs without holes in them. Just like you are hoping that she doesn't have on grannie panties, she is hoping you aren't wearing boxers with hearts or frogs on them—or ones that look like Swiss cheese.

Before you get dressed to go out, shower and put on your cologne. It should be something spicy, but not something that every man in America wears. Don't put it on your clothes; you don't want to overwhelm

anyone. But keep in mind that scent is the strongest smell connected to memory. You want her to remember you, so put it on your naked body.

Your clothes should smell like your detergent, so *make sure they are washed*. Remember ... you're going for dangerous, not disgusting. If a girl gets close enough to smell your skin, it will ignite something in her that will make her want to smell you again, and she will keep making excuses to get close. Hooray for pheromones!

If you've been smart and taken my advice up to this point, you should have some confidence and the look women want. Now it's time to go out and have some fun—get to know girls and enjoy the "single life."

Kissing

Let's be honest. If you need to read this book, you may also need to brush up on your kissing skills. That's all right, as long as you know practicing on the back of your hand doesn't really work. If the first kiss you give the "woman of the moment" sucks, she is already thinking about whether or not she wants to suffer through another one or if she should just make an excuse to leave before you drown her in your spittle.

So how do you make sure you don't suck? First, it happens with eye contact. You need to look at her like she is an angel, not a piece of meat. For a first kiss:

- Casually lift your thumb to the side of her face and caress her jaw lightly while keeping eye contact.

- Then move your hand to the back of her head and gently pull her face to yours.

- Keep your mouth closed and touch her lips with yours.

- Your bottom lip should be slightly above hers, finding that indention in between her top and bottom lip.

- Once you make initial contact, slightly open your lips and close them again.

- Don't do weird stuff because you think it's exciting—like shake your head back and forth. It just freaks people out.

- Congratulations, you're kissing.

If you want to use a little tongue after a minute or two, great—but please do so sparingly. A little goes a long way, and you should not be giving her a tonsillectomy. Tickle the middle of her tongue once or twice, and then go back to the basics.

Slobber is disgusting. If your face starts getting wet, you are doing it wrong, so take a deep breath, wipe your face discreetly, and start again. While you are kissing, you can move both hands to the back of her head and start tugging at her hair. Don't pull hard enough to rip it out; that weave was probably expensive. Do it just hard enough to let her feel the building passion. This is the fool-proof kissing method. Hopefully her hands will start wandering too.

Also, make sure your teeth are brushed or eat a breath mint before kissing because bad breath makes the girl want to vomit, not keep kissing.

Kissing maintenance:

➤ Kip your lips covered in ChapStick anytime you think about it. Dry lips are gross. You don't want her thinking about whether your lips feel more like rhino skin or tree bark; you want her getting lost in the moment.

➤ Wet your lips before kissing if you don't have ChapStick.

➤ Also, if you have trouble with your breath, brush your tongue a lot. It helps with your breath by killing excess bacteria, as does flossing and mouthwash.

This isn't rocket science; but if you are not aiming to be boyfriend material, your kisses should be on fire every single time you kiss. Also, great first kisses happen against walls or hard surfaces.*

Back her into a wall by walking closer and closer to her until her back hits the wall. Put your hand up next to her face, palm down on the wall. Give her a slow smile, and then lean in and follow all the appropriate steps. Trust me—things will become caliente!

---

*First kisses for "better things" can happen anywhere (wink, wink).

The Girlfriend

3

Okay, you've enjoyed your bachelor days, but now you're ready for something else—something more substantial than Pringles. You're ready for a girlfriend. You're ready to leave the party-boy image behind and find that "special someone." Don't race off to the nearest bar and try to find her. Start your search by actually thinking about what you are looking for. You might even be the kind of dude who makes lists, so get out your pen and paper or your iPhone notepad. Think about more than just looks here.

Here are some questions you might ask yourself: How important are looks to you really? Does she need to be straight from a magazine? Perhaps she just needs to be relatively pretty. What facial feature is most important to you? Eyes? Lips? Think about her figure. Maybe you like stick-thin girls, or perhaps you like a little junk in the trunk. Big boobs or small?

Now that you have looks out of the way, think about other qualities she needs to have since looks are going to fade over time.* Is it important to you that she

---

*Unless she is a Botox-a-holic, plastic-surgery-addict ...

is a spiritual person? Are political beliefs something that matter to you? What are your views on education? If you have a college degree, you might want her to have one too.

Is a long-distance relationship okay, or would you prefer someone a little closer to home? Are you okay with Internet dating or not?

Now make a list of yourself. Write down as many things you can think of that make you who you are. Don't write what you look like. (Duh, you already know that.) Write down things you love to do. Write down the things and people that are the most important to you. Here would be an example:

1. Christian.

2. Can't live without my motorcycles or red meat.

3. I love to fish on weekends.

4. I hate cats.

5. I love dogs.

6. I love guns.

7. My mom and sister are the most important people to me.

8. I love to travel.

9. I think Kung-Fu movies and UFC are amazing.

10. I hate shopping.

Once you have this list, you know that you are looking for someone who can live with these things about you. So when you meet a girl, if she is an anti-gun activist or a vegan, say, "Nice to meet you," and keep looking. Trust me on this one: you don't want to change yourself too much in the beginning just to have things "in common" with a woman. Down the road, you are going to resent her and be unhappy, and she is going to tell you all the time that she doesn't know who you are anymore. It will be true because you never showed her who you *really* were. Just be honest up front; but remember, if you don't know yourself and what you are looking for, you will never find it.

Now make a list of no more than five things that you can't compromise on—things you know you AREN'T looking for. If it is more than five things, you are way too picky, and you need to look inside yourself and ask why you are such a prick. (Kidding!) Once you have this list, you're good to go.

The Image:

The boyfriend image is different than the party-boy image. You might still need that one-night stand, too-cool-for-school outfit to keep the sex alive. You want her to see you like that sometimes because nothing will turn her on more than having you on her arm when every woman in the room wants you. Don't flirt with

every woman in the room when this happens though! That's a quick way to get frozen out.

Now, looking for a girlfriend is a different animal, and that animal wears khaki shorts and pants (not cargo pants) and Polo shirts. They don't have to be Polo brand, though; just a collared, two-button shirt will work with a flat-front pant or short.

Simple color rules are: Do not wear navy and black together. Do not wear brown and black together unless the brown is khaki. You will look terrible, and all night every girl will be thinking about your fashion mishap, secretly feeling a little sorry for you.

Wear a belt. If you have brown shoes, wear a brown belt. Black shoes go with a black belt. No exceptions.

Leather flip-flops are great casual wear as long as your feet aren't gross. Speaking of feet, keep your toenails short. If they have a white line at the top, cut those things! Ewww! Also, wax off or shave the hair on your toes. No one wants to date a gorilla. If you have a hairy back, same rule applies. If you aren't the flip-flop type of guy because you can't seem to get the toe-grip/walking thing down, then find a good pair of sneakers. New Balance and Adidas make great classic sneakers; but if you get solid white ones, you might as well move into the retirement home and get some denture cream.

You could even get Nike Shox; but remember when you wear any shoes with shorts, your socks shouldn't show over the shoe. You could also wear boat shoes without socks. These are great summer shoes and will go with almost anything. (And they look cool.)

If you are wearing khaki pants, then you MAY NOT wear flip flops or athletic sneakers. If you do, she is going to think you aren't manly enough, or that there is something wrong with your vision. Surely you wouldn't have left the house looking like that if you had the ability of full sight. With khaki pants, you should wear a brown or black casual shoe or loafer. Think Cole Haan or Kenneth Cole. Get on Amazon or again go to a discount store and find one with a square shape.

If you wear jeans, you can wear athletic sneakers or boots, but please don't wear flip-flops with this either. You will look like a guy who isn't trying because he partied too hard the night before.

If you are pasty white, get a tanning membership.* It's okay; men do that all the time. I see guys there almost every time I go, so don't be embarrassed. If you are embarrassed, sign up at a salon in an area you

---

*Please do not become addicted to tanning. Not only could you increase your chances of getting cancer, but you'll look ridiculous.

don't normally frequent. Things to know when you go there:

- Buy a pair of tanning goggles and get the kind without the strap so you don't get a little white line on the side of your face. (You don't want to advertise that you are fake-baking.)

- Tan naked. Just do it! It's kind of like getting a physical … it isn't fun to think about, but you need to be a man and do this for your well-being with women. Don't worry; the beds are sanitized, and you don't want an underwear line. Don't get the lotion. You'll just smell weird, and you'll end up looking like George Hamilton with orange hands.

- When you get into the bed, pull the top down. I know this sounds stupid, but you wouldn't believe how many people don't know that! (I actually didn't know that the first *three* times I went. That's embarrassing to admit, so learn from my mistakes.)

Your hair care should be the same as the party-boy, except you should shave periodically. Also, if you have weird hair in your ear or something, pluck it, wild man. Unless you're a hobbit, that just isn't a place to have sprouts of hair.

Places to Meet Your New Girlfriend:

Now that you are in the right mindset and you have the right wardrobe, you need to think about where you can meet decent women—the kind you can bring home to Mom.

The bar where you used to pick up women is out. No one meets their soul mate in a bar, and for *sure* no one wants that to be the story they tell when people ask where they met. If you are religious, you might meet someone at church. This is secretly the place where all religious women WANT to say they met you. With this one sentence, you win over every single family member and friend.

Watch it in action. When someone asks you where you met your girlfriend, say, "Oh, we met at church." I don't care who they are. They will be all smiles, compliments, and say, "Oh, we'd love to have y'all over to the house."

So obviously if you are religious and looking for someone who is also religious, start at your church. If your church doesn't have any singles your age, find a new church. But keep in mind: if you are dating a church girl, the rules are different. She is a good girl who you can't expect to be putting out all the time, as it goes against her beliefs. If church is your venue, another good piece of advice is to focus on God and

let Him do the rest. He will let you know the who and when the time is right.

Another great place to meet single women is a coffee shop, bookstore, or a combination coffee shop/bookstore. You can tell a lot about a girl depending on which section you find her in.

If she is in the art section, awesome! Artists make the most amazing girlfriends, although they can be a bit up and down. Artists are driven visually, so you should keep this in mind if you are dating them. They have ideas of beautiful moments strung together in their minds, and that is what they want. They can tend to be moody, but they can move from one mood to another quickly. You will win an artist over with grand gestures and spontaneous dates.

If she is in the poetry section, run away. She's too intense and will analyze everything you say and do until the second-coming. Should you decide to proceed with her, I hope you're intellectual. Get out your blazer with patches sewn into the elbows that will match the soul patch you'll be required to grow on your chin.

If she is in the romance or chick lit section, this is probably your girl. This girl is reading about these brooding men that somehow notice the normal heroine of their books and makes them feel like the only girl in the world. That's what she wants from you—to be noticed positively and made to feel like she is the only girl your eyes can see. She wants you to be romantic, bring her flowers, and listen to her day. She expects the heroes of the novels she is reading.

If she is in the children's book section, she either has kids of her own or has a child she is close to. If you aren't ready to treat her children like they are the most important little people in the world, move right along. Her children deserve a man who treats them like princes and princesses; and ultimately, that is what she is looking for anyway.

Use whatever section she is in as your roadmap in how to proceed.

If she is sitting alone at a coffee shop curled up with a book, or even sitting with a girlfriend, you may want to approach her, or offer to buy her the next cup. You could even use that cute line from *Friends* where Ross says, "Can I buy you a cup of coffee, or at least reimburse you for the one you have?" You better laugh after you say this and not be awkward, or else you're going to get a weird stare.*

You might meet a woman in the grocery store; but let's be honest—if you do, she has baggage, like an ex-husband and kids. There is nothing wrong with that! But if you are reading this book and you're twenty-two, that's not the place this chance meeting is going to happen. If you're thirty-two, it might be the place for you.

---

* And you should just walk away at that point.

If you meet her at a wine bar, that's different than meeting at a club or regular bar. Wine bars are fine, as are restaurant bars.

You might even meet her through mutual friends. Put out the feelers with your girl friends or guy friends' girlfriends that you are looking to be set up. Girls LOVE to play matchmaker. If you do it this way, just be ready for the girl that sets you up to feel like she is part of your relationship—and feels like she is entitled to details every step of the way. She will also take it personally if it doesn't work out, so be careful.

Then, there is online dating. I can't say I'm *opposed* to it—it's a great way to meet people, especially if you live in a small town. But here is the issue: Online dating takes the relationship out of the relationship. You don't get to meet and get to know each other. You ask each other all of the normal dating questions before you ever go on the date. Uncool.

If you are in the circumstance that you are going to be choosing your lucky lady online, I suggest after two fifteen-minute online conversations,˙ ask her to meet you for coffee. If she says no, ask her to take a chance on you in a public place. She will say yes unless she has been less-than-honest in her profile and is secretly fat or has a deformity she is hoping you

---

˙Please don't talk for hours online because there is no mystery in that, and you will be bored on your second date.

will look past after hours of getting to know her from behind your computer.

When you see a woman you want to meet, you're going to have to be bold—but you'll have to be smart at the same time. This means that you have to start approaching women, even if they are with their friends. But you also need some social awareness to know if she is giving you the "please-leave-me-alone" signal.

This is how you approach in general: First, make eye contact and smile. If she smiles back and doesn't have a ring on her finger or a man on her arm, get her on your radar. Keep your eye out for a few minutes and see who she is with and what she is doing. Make eye contact and smile a few more times. Hold her gaze, and if you do and she is still smiling instead of looking away or down, approach and introduce yourself.

If she tries not to make eye contact with you after the first time, or she keeps looking down or away, leave her alone. She is letting you know she isn't interested.

Now we all know that women are complicated. What happens if she has smiled and kept your gaze and you go over to talk to her and you're getting mixed signals? If she gives you short answers, doesn't let you in on what she has going on that day, or she

starts mentioning how she and her friend have to get somewhere, cut and run. Something has rubbed her the wrong way about you, and she is just being polite and trying to get away.

Politely tell her it was nice to meet her and you hope she and her friend have a great day. Then walk away. Don't ask for her number, remind her that you are free all day, or worse, start hitting on her friend instead. Just stop embarrassing yourself. There are millions of other women out there, and probably a few thousand of them who will think you are amazing.

Here are some good examples of things you can say and do in each meeting place to a pretty young thing that has caught your eye:

Church

Please do not hit on a girl during the service. Geez ... you should be worshipping. At least wait until the service is over. Better yet, wait until the singles group or your Sunday school group is having a fellowship time. The church girl is the hardest girl to get, but she is also the most worth it. If you already share the same values, you have it made.

Approach her if you don't already know her and introduce yourself. Be confident!

Say "Hi," hold out your hand, and give hers a light shake. Don't kiss it at church, Rico Suave. Continue with, "I'm (insert your name here), and I just realized we've never met." Paste a smile on your face and keep eye contact with her. She needs to feel like she is the only person in the room.

Conversation starters here:

- How long have you been going to church here?

- I notice you sing in the choir. I wish I could sing. Have you been talented your whole life or did you have to work at it?

- Can you tell me how I can get more involved here?

- I thought the sermon tonight was really interesting. How about you?

Things not to say:

- Wow! You must have fallen from heaven because you are an angel.

- Thank you God for answering my prayer.

- God told me we were going to get married.

- You're pretty. Want to date me?

If your conversation is going well and you seem to both have lots to say, ask her if she'd like to get coffee

with you sometime. If it's going *really* well, ask her if she'd like to continue your conversation over coffee. But if y'all are struggling for things to say, ask her if it would be okay to Facebook her or get her number to go get coffee in the next couple of days. Give her a chance to think about you a little bit, and give yourself a chance to think of more things to say.

If she says, "Sure, maybe a few of us could go together," she isn't interested in you as anything more than a brother-in-Christ, or whatever religion you are practicing. It doesn't mean she will never see you that way; but it means initially she is either not attracted to you, or she isn't looking for anything right now. This means you will have to either change her mind on your first "group date," or you will patiently wait for years on the sidelines. Trust me—if after date number two it doesn't happen, don't waste your time. If she wanted you, she would have jumped at the chance to hang out with you alone. You're setting yourself up for heartbreak if you wait for months only for her to fall in love with someone else.

Coffee Shop

If you meet her at the coffee shop and you happen to be standing next to her in line waiting for your half-caf venti triple caramel macchiato, look over at her from the side and smile. If she smiles back with her eyes AND her mouth, remark about how complicated coffee orders have gotten in the past ten years and how your grandmother would be lost in a place like this.

"Listening to them shout out coffee orders is like listening to another language!" If she smiles politely and says nothing, get your coffee and go.

If she laughs or says ANYTHING back, keep talking. Ask her, "What did you order?"

Reply with, "That sounds good. I always like to try new things," to whatever she says, unless she says something crazy like "Regular coffee."

If she does say that, laugh! Tell her that the cashier probably didn't know how to ring that up, it was so old school.

Then introduce yourself. Shake hands if you aren't holding boiling hot coffee by this point. Mention that you are going to relax at that table over there and enjoy your complicated coffee. Say, "You're welcome to join me if you aren't in a hurry."

She might actually be in a hurry, so don't take it personally if she can't. If she gives you a real reason why she can't, she probably wishes she could.

"Oh, Mike, I'd love to, but I'm actually running late to my niece's birthday party," means that she wishes she could.

"Oh, Mike, I can't. I'm already late," means she isn't really late. She just realized that you wanted to get to know her better, and she isn't interested for whatever reason. It doesn't mean you aren't attractive

or funny. She might have a boyfriend or have just gotten out of a bad relationship. Don't let this destroy your confidence. Enjoy your coffee. There might be a cute woman across the room already who is waiting for you to make eye contact.

If you see a pretty lady across the room, smile at her as you sit down and make eye contact. If she smiles back more than once and holds your gaze, walk over and try Ross's line from *Friends* or be charmingly dorky.

Tell her, "I'm a little nervous because I don't normally introduce myself to beautiful women, but I saw you sitting here and thought I'd take a chance. I'm Mike." Give her a goofy grin and a handshake. Then say, "Can I buy you another cup of coffee?"

If she says yes, great! Sit down (after getting her new coffee), and get to know her. Ask about her work, her life passions, her family, and her favorite foods.

If she says no or that she has to go somewhere, don't let it be awkward, and *don't* try to make her feel sorry for you. That's pathetic. Smile at her and say something smooth like, "Well, it was worth a shot." Then wink at her and walk away.

Bookstore

If you meet in a bookstore, please be holding a book in your hand that you are actually interested in reading so you don't look like a slimy putz who is only trying to pick up women. Also, you need an excuse to be in the chick lit section. Do your homework. Look up a popular female author (or just read the titles and authors listed below) and pretend like you are looking for one of these books for your sister/aunt/best friend because you know she likes that author and you are trying to be thoughtful. Women LOVE that.

- The *Shopaholic Series* by Sophie Kinsella

- *The Other Side of the Story* by Marian Keyes

- *Jemima J* by Jane Green

- *Everyone Worth Knowing* by Lauren Weisberger

- *Black Dagger Brotherhood* by J. R. Ward

So you are perusing the stacks, and you see a woman without a wedding ring looking in the stacks. You start looking on the same aisle. Please don't be so obvious about checking her out. Actually look in the stacks. Pick up books and put them back down. She is probably going to give you a weird look if you're in the chick lit section. Look up at her with an embarrassed smile, and then turn back and give a frustrated sigh.

Walk over to her after looking and reading the backs of the books again for a minute. If she looks at you and smiles again, go closer to her and say, "Excuse me. I know that you don't work here, but do you think I could ask you a question about all this?" Gesture

toward the multitude of womanly books, looking overwhelmed. She will probably say sure!

This is when you spin your tale of how you are trying to be a good big brother, nephew, or best friend.

"I'm really sorry to ask you this, but I'm totally lost. My sister Sarah came down with the flu, and I wanted to do something nice for her because she loves to read. So I came to get her a book, but I'm in a little over my head! I don't know where to begin."

She will say, "Oh, that's so sweet of you. Do you know what kind of books she likes?"

"I know she likes love stories and something called the Shopping Novels,˙ but I think I could use some help. Have you read any books that you would recommend?"

She will probably have a few things she can recommend, and she will likely take you there and show you what they are. You don't need to buy ten books; just pick one—but you are really going to have to buy it if you ask this helpful honey to have coffee with you as a thank you for her being so helpful.

"I'm Mike, by the way," you should throw in there as she darts off to help you find a book for your invalid sister.

˙The woman will know EXACTLY what you are talking about, but you don't want to know exactly what you are talking about, or you will seem gay.

She will most likely introduce herself too. Say something clever or amazing here so you will give her a reason to want to keep talking to you. She is already going to think you are a saint, by the way.

"Lucy, my sister is going to be eternally grateful that I didn't come back with *War and Peace* or *Louisiana Game and Fish* because of your intervention. Please, let me buy you a cup of coffee to say thank you."

If there isn't a coffee bar attached, offer to buy her a book as a thank you. Just take it out of her hand and refuse to let her pay for it. While you are signing your credit card stub, write your name and number in the cover with a little note that says you'd like to take her to dinner sometime.

Just so you know, if you do this, paperbacks are at least ten dollars. Hard back are like twenty or more—sometimes much more, so hope there is a coffee bar attached! If she has a thousand dollar book in her hand and there is no coffee shop, keep the conversation going for a minute or two or three, and then say, "I'm really enjoying talking to you, Lucy. This may seem a little forward, but I'd love to continue our conversation sometime. Would you like to meet me for coffee or lunch sometime?"

If she says yes, great! If she says no, don't worry about it. You're never going to see her again. Just don't stay and hit on someone else that day. You'll get a reputation, and the book shelving workers will

start to call you the Sick-Sister Love Bandit. That's a terrible nickname that you should avoid at all costs.

Grocery Store

If you happen to meet her in the grocery store, you are on a different playing field. It is going to be hard to not be creepy. You make one wrong move, and she has the pepper spray out and is holding on to her purse for dear life. "Accidently" meet her on more than one aisle. Wait patiently for her to get her peanut butter and then you get yours, smiling at her.

When you meet again from opposite ways on the paper towel aisle, smile at her again and say something like, "We must have the same shopping list." Let her laugh and smile. If she says something back, great! If she just smiles at you and looks down, she isn't interested.

If she gave you the smile and response, meet her again over by the milk and say something clever like, "We have to stop meeting like this," with another smile.

If she laughs again and comments, say, "I'm Mike. "Hold out your hand and ask her if she wants to walk to the checkout with you. Add an excuse about how you'd love some company in the checkout line because usually the waiting is so long and boring.

She will either say yes or tell you she has to go get toothpaste or something. This is her way of saying she isn't interested. If she says yes, enjoy the conversation about where she is from, what she does, and about what her favorite foods are. She may not be comfortable walking out to her car with you, since every Lifetime movie is about someone abducting somebody else at their vehicle in the grocery store parking lot, so don't sweat that.

As she checks out, tell her you really enjoyed getting to know her and that she made the usually-boring shopping trip much more interesting.

"Lucy, you've made buying milk so much more enjoyable than normal. I'd love to casually bump into you again sometime. Would you be up for that?"

If she says yes, go for coffee. Coffee is the least threatening date with the most ways to escape if it goes horribly wrong, but it also the potential to stretch the date out if it's good. You could also suggest ice cream or yogurt. Always suggest something with a flexible duration in case you both realize you'd rather beat your face with a 2×4 than talk to each other any longer.

If you happen to meet through friends, there is going to already be a little more pressure on the date, so it is your job to make it lighthearted.

If your best friend's girlfriend sets you up with someone, request that it be for coffee, ice cream, or yogurt. You should never go for dinner first because if you don't hit it off, you're stuck with her for two hours. And you have to pay a lot more money than just a five dollar cup of coffee.

If you are meeting online, you should have no more than two strategic conversations via email or instant messenger. They should include the basics:

➣ What do you do for a living?

➣ What are you interests?

➣ Do you like sports?

➣ What kinds of foods do you like?

➣ Would you be interested in taking a chance and meeting me for coffee?

If you can't tell, I'm not the biggest fan of online dating, again, because it takes so much of the mystery out of dating. When you actually go on a date, you'll have already said everything there is to say online! Yikes! Keep the mystery alive online and get her to meet you in person to walk your dogs or play miniature golf. If she lives six hours away, that might not be so doable, so be realistic when looking for someone online and try to find someone close to your area.

Twenty-Five Easy Second Dates

I cannot say this enough: First dates should be coffee, yogurt, or ice cream. They should be in a public place with plenty of exits without a lot of time commitment. Basically first dates should be in a place where you can focus on each other. How will you know if you want a second date when you can't talk to her? The movies are for the third or fourth date because at that point, you don't have to do quite so much talking to know you get along well.

Here are some sure-fire ideas for second dates, and some of them are totally free! Keep in mind that if you really want to get in good and score a lot of brownie points with her, remember something that she said she liked during your first date and bring it to her. Maybe she mentioned that she loves Junior Mints, flowers, or reading. Bring her a single flower from your yard, a box of her favorite candy, or a book from the book-store that you think she might like. Burn a CD of songs you think she might like. It doesn't have to be expensive; it just has to show her that you actually

listened to the things she said on your first date and you cared enough to take the time to show her that.

She will be over the moon and decide right then and there that YOU are a keeper! Just don't do something weird like write her a poem or tell her that you had a dream about the two of you getting married ... or worse, buy her lingerie. She will think you are a creepy, clingy horn dog, and that is not the way to her heart or her panties.

One thing that all women are looking for is a gentleman. This means you should call her at least two days ahead for the date. It gives her a chance to anticipate and get excited about it, and it lets her know that she wasn't your last minute thought. Show her you actually took time to plan this. Don't believe me? There are probably a hundred books out there telling women that if you call her or text her and invite her to do something that day, you didn't put any thought into it, and she was a last minute decision or choice. Those books tell her to say no to you because you weren't thoughtful enough. Show her that she is worth planning ahead and you respect her schedule. Be the gentleman who asks her if she is free on Thursday evening because you have something special planned. Don't be the douche who texts her with "R U free 2nite?"

If possible, pick her up at her house. Do not call her from the car to meet you in the driveway, you jerk. Get your lazy butt out of the car and ring her doorbell. If she lives with her parents, go in, look her father in the eye, and shake his hand. Bring flowers for her AND for her mother. Then, walk her to the passenger side of the car and open up the door for her. Have light music playing so it's not constant awkward silence, but a comfortable ride.

When you arrive at your destination, open her car door and then open the door for her wherever you decide to go. If you are in a restaurant, treat the service staff well and leave them a decent tip. That means twenty percent. And remember, you are the man. *You* pay for dinner. If you cannot afford to pay for dinner, don't ask her out for a dinner date. Cook for her at home or do something free like a hike in the park. Any guy who ever gave me the awkward stare when the waiter asked if we were paying together or separate, I immediately erased from my phone and ditched. She is worth the twelve dollar pasta.

If you offer to go Dutch, you might not ever see this woman again, like my experiences, or those experiences of any other woman I know. If she offers to pay, you refuse. As a matter of fact, if you hesitate for one second when the waiter asks you that question and make her feel like she needs to offer, you are not a gentleman and have not done your job. Shame on you!

If, however, she starts to feel bad that you are always paying, and she calls you up to ask you on

a date and insists on paying, this is okay—but only every once in a blue moon, and not out to the nicest place in town.

When you end your date, walk her to her door. Don't just wait in the car for her to get in safely. Take her to the door no matter what, even if you had an awful time.

And if you want to be cute in a dorky way, call her as soon as you get in your car and say, "Hi Lucy. I just wanted to call you to tell you I had a really great time tonight, and I can't stop thinking about you." She is going to laugh at you because you are probably still in her driveway, but it will endear you to her. Don't stay on the phone! This should be a fifteen second call.

"I know I'm still in your driveway, but I just had to call you and see if we could do something again soon, like Monday night. What do you think?"

It's cute. You can't do this every date, but you can do it after the first or second one. You should call her the day after every date in the beginning to tell her you had a great time on your date the night before and that you would love to do it again sometime. Ask what day she would be free this week. Again, this tells her that you know her plans and schedule are just as important as yours.

One classic dating mistake is that couples tend to get stuck in a rut. Dinner, movies, movies, dinner, and making out on the couch. While I'm sure she will enjoy your company no matter what you choose to do, try to mix it up to keep the relationship exciting. There will be plenty of time for boring down the road … trust me, I have been married. I'm not saying don't have an easy night in, but try to only do that once a week. Have an exciting date once a week too. Here are some ideas:

Dog Walking at the Park

If she is an animal lover, ask her if she wants to take her dog for a walk in a local park. Surprise her by packing a picnic for the two of you—and bring mosquito spray! After you've been walking for a little while, tell her that you wanted to surprise her with a picnic and lead her to a shady spot. Here are some easy things you can make, even if you only know how to maneuver a microwave.

Buy some chicken salad in the deli section of the grocery store and spread it on wheat bread. Grab some chips and some mixed fruit in clear containers in the produce section. You should also bring two bottles of water and maybe even buy some Milano cookies. You might want to pack two peanut butter and jelly sandwiches too, in case she hates chicken salad. Don't forget to bring plastic forks to eat the fruit with, and if you really want to win her over, pack some treats and some water for her dog. Put it all in an ice chest or tote. There is no reason you as a man should own a

picnic basket. Also, you should bring a blanket for the two of you to sit on so neither of you get ants in your pants. Stripping down is never a bad thing, but not for that reason.

Just a Picnic

I know I keep pushing the picnic idea, but it goes a long way even if you don't want to combine it with pets. I suppose my reasoning is that the date that really won me over with my ex-husband was a picnic. I was at work, and I had an hour lunch break. He showed up at my office and surprised me, taking me to the lakefront near my office building. He had a large, brown-handled bag filled with delicious food and a blanket thrown over one arm. He wouldn't even let me help set up the blanket! He wanted me to just relax. When we sat down, he laid out paninis he had made using a George Foreman grill, chips, fresh-cut pineapple, water bottles with fruit and ice at the bottom, and cupcakes. He was obviously an advanced picnicker, and I will always remember that this was the moment I decided to give him a real shot.

If you are going on a picnic, you should tell her to wear comfortable shoes if possible, unless you're going on an urban picnic like I did. Take her on a short hike on a well-worn trail and find a river or creek to stop by. If the picnic is the main attraction, not a rushed lunch date on a work day, you are going to have to step up your game! You might want to ask a woman in your life for some help with special touches, but you don't have to.

You should make this meal great by serving fresh-cut fruit, assorted cheeses and crackers,* sandwiches or cold chicken, and some homemade cookies. If you really want to wow her, bring sparkling cider in clear plastic cups and drop a strawberry or raspberry into her cup as you serve it. Or you can put fruit and ice into big clear water bottles because it will be amazingly refreshing. You should bring hot chocolate if it is cold outside. Make a toast to her agreeing to go on a second date with you and to her being the most special woman you know.

Again, you should have bug spray and a picnic blanket. If you bring a basket, make a point to say that you borrowed it from your grandmother. Perhaps you could even bring two books or magazines for you both to lay back and read.

Encourage her to lay back with you and point out shapes in the clouds. That's fun and a chance for the two of you to get closer physically. If she starts moving around a lot, it's time to pack it in and go home because (a) she has been sitting on a tree root

---

*You could buy one of the trays at Wal-Mart, disassemble it, and put it all into separate containers, pretending like you put it all together yourself.

and quietly enduring it, or (b) she is getting eaten alive by the bugs of the forest and doesn't want to ruin your date by saying so.

Volunteering at the Animal Shelter

Girls like guys who like animals. I always felt that someone who doesn't like animals isn't trustworthy. If she sees you treating a helpless animal well, she will automatically think you are going to treat her well too. Call ahead to an animal shelter and ask if they could use two volunteers on Saturday. Then tell your new love interest that you are going to pick her up at 8 am on Saturday and to wear clothes she can get dirty!* Take her and bond over the cute fluffy-eared dogs! End your date by playing with all of the little puppies, and you will melt her heart. Then tell her, "I know I just met you and all, but there is something I've wanted to tell you all day. You smell like wet dog!" Then laugh. Keep it fun and playful, and you will enjoy seeing a smile on her face that lasts all afternoon. See if she wants to get cleaned up and get coffee again later if you had a great time together. I bet that while she is getting cleaned up, she will also be texting her friends and updating her Facebook status with "best date ever!"

---

* (Please make sure she isn't afraid of dogs or anything. If she was attacked as a small child, then this date would be disastrous.)

Going to a Sporting Event

Ask her if she wants to go to the local adult league soccer game. Don't ask her to go to a kids' game if you don't have a child or nephew playing. That's creepy. But otherwise, ask away. Bring popcorn and choose opposite teams to root for. It's way more fun if you are cheering for opposites. Make a friendly bet that if her team loses, she has to help wash your car; but if *your* team loses, you will take her out for a nice dinner. No one really loses there!

If you go to a big game with a professional team, the same principles apply, but there will be minor differences. Fans are more hardcore here. If anyone is rude to her, or is cursing near her, stand up for your lady! Don't get in a fight, for heaven's sake. She likes your nose where it is. Just nicely ask the offender to tone down his loud cursing in front of the ladies, or whatever the situation calls for. If the offender does not apologize, back down immediately and walk away. She will admire you for trying, and she will admire you for not getting into a fight. It does take a stronger man to walk away, and that in itself is sexy.

Also at a major sporting event, don't complain about the price of the food. Yes, it's a seven dollar hot dog. Get over it. Complaining about the cost of things will make your date uncomfortable. Instead, take the

time to explain the game to her. Things will be loud, so it will give you a chance to get closer!

Go to an Art Gallery or Museum

It is usually around ten dollars to go to either of these places, and you will have lots of things to look at and comment on. Perhaps you both find yourself getting a little bored. Tell her that you'd love to take a break in the museum café and order two desserts. Share them both and comment on how much you love a woman who eats dessert.

Or, go to the museum gift shop, look around for a minute, and say, "Nope. There is nothing as beautiful as you are in this whole place! Not even the Van Gogh!" She will laugh and smile and call you crazy, but she will secretly love that you said it. If you really want to be Mr. Amazing, pick up a post card from the gift shop. Tell her it is because you like the picture or you want a little something to remember the date by. Then when you get home, write on it how much fun you had on your date. Tell her the most interesting thing you saw that day was her. Sign it and mail it to her. Don't say ANYTHING about it until she brings up that she received it.

If you both hate art and culture, this could still be fun. Take two notepads and pens with you and have a competition about who can make the snarkiest or most sarcastic comments about the pieces you see that day. Compare notes in the café afterward, but still do the postcard thing because it's awesome.

Picture Scavenger Hunt

Meet at a local park or other public location and hand her a disposable camera.* Tell her that you are both going on an adventure today, but there is a catch. You each have 24 chances to take the most interesting pictures of the strangest things you can find. Then open the car door for her and set off. Decide on a place to stop, which could be the mall parking lot or even a bowling alley. Have a great time until you both run out of film. Take them cameras to Walgreens and get them developed. It'll take about an hour, so have fun exploring the store's treasures.† Then take the pictures to Starbucks and go over them one by one. It doesn't really matter who wins! You'll have the best time laughing over the pictures you took, but if you want to be a gentleman, you should let her win. Choose one of hers that is the best, and pick one of yours to be runner up. Make sure that you've taken a picture of her and ask her if she minds if you keep it. Don't tell her why; just tell her you like that one and want to

---

*Yes, they still sell disposable cameras. It'll be more fun than using your cell phone—the anticipation of how your pictures turn out will be fun!

†Don't have too much fun ... you don't want to get kicked out of the store!

keep it. She will smile and say yes and be secretly so excited if she finds that picture on your bedside table one day. Please don't be redneck about it and put it on your dashboard.

Bowling

I don't care who you are; bowling is fun! Go rent some shoes, choose outrageous names to put on your scorecards, and ask for her advice on how to choose a bowling ball. She will probably pick the prettiest one. Order pizza and beer for your date and have a great time throwing the ball down the lane. Teach her how to do it and cheer her on. Make a bet on who wins—and make it something fun. Competition always makes things fun as long as it is lighthearted. If you are the kind of person who is a sore loser, stay away from competitive things around her because that's not a good quality to show her. If you lose, tell her you want to redeem yourself by seeing who can eat their pizza the fastest.

Then go buy her something out of the 25 cent machine—and be really cheesy about it. Come back with a serious expression on your face. Dramatically sit down, and say, "Lucy, I know this is only our second date, but I wanted to get you something special to commemorate this moment." Then pull out the mood ring or bouncy ball and have a good laugh. Girls like humor! You can be challenged in the looks arena; but if you're funny and you make her laugh, you instantly become cuter to the woman of your dreams.

Fishing

If you invite her to go fishing, it cannot be the man-fishing-marathon like you would do with your buddies. I'm telling you right now—that has disaster written all over it! Girls do not want to pee in the woods or anywhere else except for a real bathroom. Also, you need to bring the easiest fishing pole known to man, and you're going to have to bait her hook every single time. Otherwise, her line will get tangled up every cast, and she will scream and squeal when she has to touch the worms and kill them painfully. And heads up: she is not going to want to touch the fish either, and that's okay. Don't be annoyed by her womanly side. Focus on getting to know her; and know that while she is squealing about how slimy the fish is, she wants you to be the man and do all of the manly stuff which will only make you more attractive in her eyes. She will reward you for making this easier for her later, I'm sure.

Things to bring:

- Two chairs
- An ice chest with drinks, sandwiches, and snacks
- Bug spray

This is really just another chance for you two to get to know each other. It is not a fishing tournament for you. After two hours of sweating outside, being eaten by bugs, and no bathroom in sight, she will be ready to go home whether she says so or not. So make a deal. Say, "I'm ready to go eat these fish! What if we make a deal? Let's go back to my place, I'll clean the fish, and we can cook them together. What do you think?"

Or, if you didn't catch anything, offer to buy her dinner at a local seafood restaurant since the whole catching your own dinner thing didn't work out. Of course, you should both go home and shower first because you smell gross.

Painting With A Twist

More than likely, you have a place in your town like I do called Painting with a Twist—or at least something like that. It's a store where you can each pay about thirty-five dollars to paint a masterpiece. You don't actually have to know how to paint, so don't worry. It's more of a paint-by-numbers thing that is cool to do together, and you can bring a bottle of wine with you. Wine is always a plus and so is and getting to know each other better while laughing at your lack of artistic ability.

The Dollar Store Date

Take her to the Dollar Tree, give her twenty dollars, and tell her to go crazy. Both of you can buy the dumbest things imaginable and come up with fun things to do with them that day. You can dress up like superheroes, have sword fights, eat cheap candy, and buy strange fake plants to decorate your place with. Jokingly call it your "love fern," like from the movie *How to Lose a Guy in Ten Days*. Make sure you take pictures using what you bought later together.

Cooking Dinner

If you are looking for a third date or later activity, and you're serious about this girl, watch some YouTube videos and cook her dinner. Use real plates, please—no paper products with the exception of napkins should be allowed.

Go to Wal-Mart and get a set of matching plates and silverware along with drinking glasses. Go and buy two steaks, get the Idahoan instant bag of potatoes (brand is important here), some green peas, and some crescent rolls. Buy a bottle of wine or at least some cold Coke. Don't forget to pick up desert in the bakery.

You're a man. If you can't cook a steak, shame on you. YouTube it. The potatoes are microwavable. Just add some sour cream to them once they are cooked, and they taste homemade. Cook the peas in the microwave for two minutes, but add some butter and seasoning to them before they go in. Follow the oven directions on the bread, and you are set!

Light some candles in the middle of the table. Go to the Dollar Tree and buy a couple packs of 6 white candles and scatter them all over your table and house. Turn out the lights and wow her with the setting. When you are finished, refuse to let her do the dishes! Instead, turn on some sexy music and ask her to dance with you. Then you can make out like crazy kids. Or you can relax and "watch" a movie.

Backyard Playland

Turn your backyard into a wonderland! If you live in an apartment, hijack your parents' or a really good friend's yard. You are going to need a lot of things, but they don't have to be overly expensive, and you don't have to use all of these ideas. Things to remember about this date: Make sure she KNOWS she will be getting dirty beforehand—really dirty. Also, make sure she doesn't have anything to do later that day, because it will take her a while to get cleaned up. Request that she bring a totally new change of clothes (undergarments included) with her, and anything she might need to take a shower. Then make sure your bathroom is clean. Nothing says "I can't see myself with this guy long-term" like finding mold in your shower and facial hair in the sink. She should not feel like she needs to wear shower shoes in your bathroom. Now back to the backyard wonderland ...

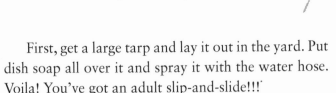

First, get a large tarp and lay it out in the yard. Put dish soap all over it and spray it with the water hose. Voila! You've got an adult slip-and-slide!!!*

➡ Get another tarp and lay out an assortment of soft foods like Twinkies and Ding Dongs, as well as bottles of ketchup and whipped cream on it. You could even have silly string, although it isn't technically a food. This is the food fight station; and as long as your date is dressed right, she will find herself having fun, and you will get an excuse to touch her, tackle her, and pour ketchup into her hair. You may need goggles at this station, so be prepared.

➡ Have a bucket full of water balloons that you have already filled up, as well as two Super Soaker water guns. You can have a water fight after you have your food fight, so you get a little cleaner.

➡ Have a snack station. Have foods that you might find at a real carnival like corn dogs, nachos, popcorn, candy, and some soft drinks.

This kind of date is SO much fun, but make sure before you do it that you test the waters a little bit.

---

*You could actually do this without a date because it is just so awesome.

On your first date, you could say, "Have you ever had a food fight?" Ask her if she has ever wanted to. Make sure she is a semi-active person. If she is a couch potato, this might not be her thing. Make sure you know enough about her to know she would like this.

The snack station should be the last station you go to; and when you do, settle down a little and get the conversation started by asking thought-provoking questions.

- "Lucy, who out of anyone you know is the least likely to want to have a food fight or slip and slide?"

- "Really? Why do you think that is?"

- "What do you think the craziest thing your inhibited friend would ever do?"

- "Who do you know that would love to do this?"

- "Really? Next time, maybe you and I can do something like this together and invite our friends. Would you be up for that?"

This is a great thing to say to let her know that you aren't trying to steal her away from her friends, but that you want to welcome them into your life with open arms.

One thing you need to keep in mind while you are eating is that the food is going to dry on you and start itching, so you may not have the longest conversation.

Be considerate and offer her the shower first. Don't let her sit there miserable without saying anything. Be a gentleman and tell her to go get clean!

And should she invite you in, wash her hair for her. She secretly wants you to. However, don't just assume she wants you to shower with her. Wait for the invitation or watch your hard work be wasted for being too pushy.

Broom Hockey

Ask her if she would like to come over for a date on your driveway. Don't tell her what you are doing; let her be intrigued! Tell her to wear workout clothes, but promise that you are not going for a run or anything.

Go to the dollar store and buy two brooms, a tennis ball, and a stick of chalk. Draw a goal at each end of the driveway and make a scoreboard.

When she gets to your house, if you haven't done the gentlemanly thing and picked her up, tell her that you are going to play a mean game of broom hockey. The first one to five has to buy the other person ice cream. (Really, you are going to buy the ice cream. You're the man. You pay. End of story. How many times can I say this?)

Make sure to have some cold water ready for break time—and be gentle. You don't want to stab her with the broom handle or anything! If, however, an accident does happen, use this opportunity to show

her what a great caretaker you are. Give her a bag of ice. Make a fuss over her. Insist that she lie on the couch and wait on her hand and foot. Bottom line, you should make her feel special when she is hurt.

Hopefully, she doesn't get hurt, and you get to enjoy ice cream and talk about how much fun your creative date was!

Blind Cookie-Decorating Contest

Call her and tell her to come over and to bring two scarves or blindfolds. Make sure you mention that the blindfolds are not for anything sinister. Your job is to get the ingredients to bake and decorate cookies or a cake. Here is what you need:[BL]

- 1 Bag of sugar cookie mix

- Vegetable oil

- Eggs

- Bowl, spoon, and cookie sheet

- Non-stick spray for cookie sheet

For decorating, just go into the baking aisle of your local grocery store and grab two bottles of white cookie icing and an assortment of sprinkles and stuff.

Also, pick up a gift bag and a $10 iTunes gift card or something like that.

---

*But maybe they can be later if you're lucky!!!

When she comes over, tell her that you thought the two of you could bake cookies together. Tell her that whoever decorates the best one gets what is in the gift bag. Have the bag somewhere visible but out of reach.

She is going to ask you what is in the bag, but don't tell her! While the cookies are baking, play Go Fish, Checkers, or Tic-Tac-Toe.

After the cookies have cooled off (another ten minutes off of the pan), ask her to get the scarves or blindfolds she brought. Then, lay out all of the decorating stuff you bought and tell her that the two of you are going to have a contest to see who can decorate the best cookie. I bet she will be feeling like she has this in the bag, because girls are more coordinated when it comes to that sort of thing than men. Tell her though that there is a catch! You will be doing it blindfolded. Set a timer on your phone or watch for five minutes, and then go! It is going to be a huge mess but tons of fun. When the timer goes off, admire your handiwork and laugh about it a lot. Decide on a winner (which is *her* of course) and then pop some popcorn, put the cookies on a plate, and watch a movie together while you enjoy your masterpieces!

Scavenger Hunt

This date is going to require a little outside help. Ask a good friend or relative to put together a scavenger hunt for the two of you. Pick her up at her house and

then meet your friend at their house. They will give you a series of clues; and once you get to the end, perhaps the prize is a little picnic area all set up for the two of you and some movie or miniature golf passes.

You don't want to overdo it. Have five to seven clues, otherwise it's just tedious! Each clue should be a short riddle. This isn't "National Treasure," so keep them simple and legal. If you can't figure it out, tell your friend you get one free pass and call in for help. This should be a lot of fun, and you'll learn how well you work together (or you will see if you don't).

The Rewind Date

Okay, I know we all watch DVDs and Netflix now, but back in the days of the VCR and Billy Idol, we had a rewind button. That's the whole idea of this date! During this date, you will start at the end.

Have your good night kiss first! Then, take her out for after-dinner coffee. Then go out to eat and order dessert. You will probably get a weird look from your server, but let them in on what you're doing and you'll probably get better service because they will be intrigued and think you're a cute couple.

Next order your dinner and of course, finish off the meal with an appetizer. Be sure to tip your server well! Take your date home and walk her to her door. You might even get to kiss her again after a fun and innovative date like this!

Scrapbook Date

Okay, I know this sounds super girly—and it kind of is— but you want to date this girl, don't you? So then suck it up and make the memories. She'll love this one. Take a camera and go around town taking random pictures of each other. Jump off benches or stairs and get some mid-air shots. Sneak that bad boy camera into Wal-Mart and take a picture driving their forklift or hopping on a pogo-stick. Cuddle up to a statue or two. Try to get at least one picture together that a nice passerby (who doesn't think you two are nuts) will take for you.

Get them developed in the one-hour photo center in Wal-Mart. While you wait, peruse their scrapbook section. You can get one of those all-inclusive kits for about twenty dollars. Pick up your pictures and go back to your house. Order a pizza and make a scrapbook titled "Our Crazy Day!" Make it as funny as possible by giving yourselves fake mustaches and crazy hair or superimposing her face onto Slash's body. Then, let her hold onto the scrapbook. She will go home and show it to all of her friends, telling them how great you are.

Drive-In Movie Date

Obviously, and unfortunately, there are no longer drive-in theaters in every town—or almost any town for that matter. That doesn't mean you can't recreate the feel of this date. This is a super-romantic evening date. Rent a projector or borrow one to set up in your

backyard. Play an old black-and-white movie like *Casablanca* or *Roman Holiday* on the screen. Use your iPod speakers to make sure you can both hear it. (If a projector is unavailable, you can use a laptop as a last resort, but get additional speakers.)

This movie date is about ambience. If you are amazingly creative, get twinkle lights from your local hardware store or your parent's garage and hang them all over your backyard. (Get the clear ones, not the colored ones). Then, create an outdoor bed with several sleeping bags covered in pillows and blankets. Go to Walgreens or CVS and get an assortment of candy, popcorn, and sodas. If you live in an area with tons of mosquitoes, get some repellent and some citronella candles to keep the bloodsuckers at bay.

Then, text her pictures of your handiwork and invite her over for a "back-in-time" good time. Finally, lay back, relax, and enjoy the movie and the pretty lady on your arm. She will talk about this date for the rest of her life.

"Kidnap" Your Date!

Let her roommates or parents in on the secret before you do this so that they don't call the police on you or taze you. Nothing spoils a date like handcuffs and a thousand volts of electricity coursing through your body.

Ask someone to help you get her outside if you can, and wear all black and a ski mask. When she comes outside, run out from behind the bushes and pick her up! Blind fold her and put her in your truck or car (Carefully read the last part. I did *not* say the *trunk* of your car). You may want to borrow a car from a friend so she doesn't see your car—or at least park down the street. Once you do this, gauge the situation. If she is crying and hyperventilating, immediately let her know that it's you and that she is totally safe—you just wanted to surprise her with your date.

However, if she is totally cool, play it up and disguise your voice. Tell her not to take off her blindfold until you get there. Then, pick her up and carry her over to a picnic blanket in the middle of a park or secluded woods. Just enjoy the relaxing time after something so dramatic! If you're creative, bring a sketchpad. If not, bring a coloring book.

To make this date even more awesome, get your most outrageous friend to dress up in drag and come recite poetry to you or do a choreographed break dance to the song "I'm Too Sexy." Make sure you take pictures for blackmail purposes later. This is a surefire way to have something to talk about for the next ten dates!

The Map Quest

Pack a lunch and get out a map of your state. Draw a circle in red around all of the places that are within two hours of where you are. Hang that map on the wall and let her throw a dart at it. Wherever that dart lands

within the giant red circle is where you are headed. It might be the middle of a field or a podunk town. Either way, you two will make it special and fun!

Child's Play

Invite her over to have a kid's day. Do all the fun stuff that you used to do as kids. Start off watching cartoons and eating Lucky Charms or some equally sugary amazing cereal in your pajamas. Then, get dressed and go to the zoo. Make sure you bring quarters for the petting zoo so you can feed the animals! Get your faces painted and take pictures with the cool animals.

Then go home and eat an entire box of popsicles and make picture frames or birdhouses out of the sticks. Climb the tree in your backyard and hang your birdhouse. Or carve your names into the tree and nail the picture frame up there with a picture of the two of you (inside a Ziploc bag). ·

Then, when darkness falls, go ding-dong-ditching.˙ The two of you go ring peoples' doorbells then run away and hide so no one is there when they open the door. It's stupid, I know, but it's still tons of fun!!! You will laugh like maniacs, I promise. Just don't get caught!

˙If you have no idea what that means, you've lived a sheltered life, and I'm sorry.

Game Night

Game Night is all about the snacks. You can't throw pretzels in a bowl and call it a day. Go big or go home! If you can't cook to save your life, don't worry. Get Chinese take-out or a bunch of frozen appetizers[†] and have them out on the table, along with Checkers, a deck of cards for Go Fish, Jenga, Guess Who, and any other games from Wal-Mart that sound like a great time for two people. Monopoly is not going to be one of those games. Two-player Monopoly sucks, and it takes like ten hours.

If you have an iPad or iPhone, download air hockey and Family Feud too. Play games and keep score until the two of you are mentally exhausted. Let the night's winner pick out a movie to watch. Game Night is a classic for a reason.

The Seventy Dollar Date

Save up seventy dollars and go get a gift card to Dillard's, JCPenny's, or DSW shoes for sixty dollars. Then pick her up and say, "Lucy, I know I've brought you flowers before, and I liked bringing them to you. What I didn't like was that the flowers died after about a week. I want you to have something from me that you love and can keep—like shoes. I know women love shoes!"

[†] Do me a favor and cook the wings and mozzarella sticks before you serve them to her.

Wait for a minute while she goes from flabbergasted to singing your praises. Then hand her the gift card and take her to the mall or Marshalls or wherever you got the gift card to pick out one perfect pair of shoes. She will think you are the BEST! Let her try on several pair and rate them from one to ten. Then line up all the pairs she is deciding between next to each other and pick a winning pair. Treat it like a pageant or sporting event, and you are the announcer.

With the ten dollars you have leftover, go buy the two of you pretzels in the food court and people-watch for the next hour. She will be Facebooking your amazingness before she even gets home; and every time she wears those shoes, she will remember how incredible you are.

Victory Garden Mud Fight

Okay, you're a man, so you don't really need to call this a victory garden. Pick her up and take her to a local nursery.* Tell her you thought it would be fun to plant a vegetable garden in your yard (or her yard if you don't have one). Get a shovel and two pairs of gloves. Check with a sales associate to let you in on what else you might need to make this a success. Then, the two of can you pick out a few things you would like to grow, like tomatoes and cucumbers.

---

*This nursery should be full of plants, not babies.

Spend the afternoon planting them. When you finish, you might want to take the opportunity to have a mud fight because anytime you get to get dirty together and then wet together is a good thing, and you'll have the mud right there.

Hopefully you will still be together when the veggies start sprouting. If not, enjoy the veggies your garden yields—or at least enjoy giving them to your mom so she can make something for you.

Snorkeling

If you live somewhere with lovely water, take her snorkeling in the beautiful ocean. If you are like most people though, and you are landlocked, you can still do this! Borrow a friend's pool for the afternoon and set up funny stuff on the bottom like a fake plastic plane crash, plastic sharks, and plastic fish. Get masks and snorkels too.

Put on your best Aussie accent and tell her about all the exciting animals she is going to see today, and about a plane crash that was thought to have happened in this general area. You could even make the lost city of Atlantis. Have fun splashing around in the pool and "discovering" all the treasures.

Once you have done a few or all of the things on this list, you are going to be at a point in your

relationship where you can relax a little bit. She will start suggesting things that the two of you can do together, and movie theater dates can be added into the mix. It is just so important in the beginning of your relationship that you don't take the easy road and become lazy. If you make things fun and exciting, she will want to keep dating you to see what you're going to do next!

It's kind of like school. School was always great the first two or three days because you got to know a new routine, and you had new teachers to get to know as well. After the first few days though, it became boring unless you were lucky enough to have one amazing teacher. You knew that class was going to be awesome because you never knew what to expect. When your date doesn't know what to expect, but she knows that things have been fun and exciting so far, she'll want to keep going out with the fun, exciting guy—*you!* Lazy is for later, so spend your energy being creative in the beginning. It's a bigger return on the investment.

Meeting the Important People

At this point, your girl should feel both safe and important in your life. So what's the next step? Usually it's meeting the important people in each others' lives. First, you introduce her to your best friend Larry—the gamer who has never spoken to a woman other than his mother. Then she introduces you to Sophie—the shopaholic maniac with the high-pitched, nasally voice.

You don't have to love her friends, and she doesn't have to love yours. You just all need to act civil toward each other. However, don't tell her you don't like her best friend!

Tell her you think her best friend is great, even if she is the most annoying person you've met since the day you were born until now. This is why you can lie here: Sophie has been her best friend for ten years. She has seen men come and go out of your lady love's life and listened to her complain about every single one of them. Sophie has been the one to come over with ice cream and chick flicks after the break-ups. Bottom

line, Sophie isn't going anywhere. She will be the maid of honor in your wedding and a frequent house guest in the years to come if things work out for you and your girlfriend. If you love your girlfriend, you need to accept her friends because they are an extension of her, and they always will be.

Women are not like men. Your best friend Larry might not like your girlfriend; but if he said he didn't like her to your face, you probably wouldn't listen— or you might even get a little angry and start bashing Larry's face in. He'd apologize, and it'd be done, over—finito.

If Sophie tells your girlfriend why she doesn't like you, your girlfriend is going to listen. And every time you have an argument, your girlfriend is going to call Sophie—and any other friends she has—and tell them everything you did wrong. And then Sophie is going to restate all the reasons why she doesn't like you and say, "I told you so!"

This may not seem fair to you since *you* would never discuss your relationship with anyone but her, but this is the way women are built. They need to talk about their problems to their friends. It isn't because they are looking for advice; they usually make their own decisions, but they like to bounce ideas off their friends.

Another fact about the female species is that they just want to be heard. Accept the fact right now that she is either telling her friends how great you are, or she is telling them how awful you are. She will never be silent about the relationship, so try your hardest to make it so that she is telling them how great you are. Eventually, they will be won over if you go with that tactic.

Keeping that in mind, if you and Sophie don't hit it off the first time you meet, make an extra effort. Tell your girlfriend that you KNOW how important Sophie is to her.

"Lucy, I know how important your best friend is in your life. I also know she and I had a rocky start, but I want to make up for that and try again with Sophie. Would you mind if I took Sophie out for coffee one day this week so she can get to know me a little better and ease any fears she might have about me dating you?"

Your girlfriend will swoon if you say this, and then she will probably want to make out with you or show you the lingerie she just bought. That might be all it takes. You may never actually have to go for coffee with Annoying Sophie because Sophie will get a phone call that day from your girlfriend informing her of what you just offered to do, and Sophie might change her mind about you right then and there.

Or you might have to go …

If you *do* have to court your girlfriend's best friend, tread carefully. If you go overboard, she might think you're hitting on her. BAD IDEA! Ask if she would like

to meet you there. It's not a date, so you aren't going to pick her up unless she doesn't have transportation.

You are, however, going to buy her coffee or tea or water. You are going to pull her chair out for her, and you are going to be polite no matter what she says. If you are on the friend-courtship-coffee meeting, it's because she doesn't like you and you are trying to change her mind. It also means that if you screw it up, she is going to get on the phone the second you leave with your girlfriend and say, "Ughh, I hate your boyfriend. Can you believe what he said?" And then she will embellish (kind of like you do with fishing).

Don't give her an inch. If she tells you about all the men that came before you, smile politely. She is trying to say something to make you mad enough to stop dating her friend. Maybe she wants to set her friend up with someone else. Maybe she is afraid of losing her friend to you and sees you as a threat. Or maybe the two of you just didn't click, and she is worried for her friend. If the latter is the case, consider this a good thing that she is watching out for someone you both care about.

This is an example of a conversation you might have:

You: I'm so glad you came here to meet me today, Sophie.

HER: No problem.

You: I wanted to talk to you about Lucy. Like I told her, I know you and I didn't really hit it off when we met the other day. But I also know that you are a huge part of Lucy's life, and it is important to her that you and I get along. Maybe the two of us could start over?

HER: Sure, I guess.

You: As her best friend, I know I need your stamp of approval to have a shot, Sophie. Are there any questions that you have for me about my intentions with Lucy? Or is there any advice you can give me since you've known her for so long?

By giving her an open-ended question, she gets a chance to get whatever is bothering her off her chest. She might not take the chance, but at least she's had the opportunity.

Whatever advice she gives you or concerns she poses, address them politely and don't become defensive. If you do, you've ruined any progress you've made, and your girlfriend will suffer because of it. Take the time to really get to know her friend. Ask her about her family, her job, her hobbies, and her interests. And after about thirty minutes, thank her so much for taking the time to meet with you. Tell her you are looking forward to all of you getting together

again. Hold the door for her when she leaves and smile when you tell her goodbye.

Then sit back and wait for your girlfriend to be excited about the progress the two of you have made!

However, don't expect your girlfriend to do the same thing with your guy friends. It's not fair, I know. If she mentions that she doesn't like it when Weird Larry hangs out with the two of you, GENTLY remind her that you do things with her friends too. You can suggest that she try to get to know Larry better, like you did with Sophie. If she is reasonable, then she will give him a shot after you explain that he doesn't have the best social skills. If not, you may consider it a red flag in your relationship.

Remember, in a relationship, it's good to have time away from each other too. You want to keep spending time with your friends so that your personality doesn't get lost. We all know those people who start dating, and then we never see them again. You secretly wonder if they've gone off and joined a cult of Snuggie-wearing, long-bearded tree huggers. Don't be that couple!

Beyond meeting her friends and getting their stamps of approval, you've got to meet the parents and any siblings that your new love has. Talk about intimidating! It doesn't have to be intimidating if you do your homework ... and relax.

I'm not talking about smoking-a-joint-or-drink-ing-a-forty kind of relaxing! Do that and you're toast. Just take some deep breaths and remember that this girl likes you enough to bring you home. It means you're a real contender. I never brought a boyfriend home unless I thought he was worthy of meeting my family and that we might be in it for the long-haul. When I brought my future husband through the door, my parents knew he was the real deal—before him, I hadn't brought anyone home in about two years.

So you're going to meet the parents ... what is the homework that I mentioned earlier? Here it is: find out about her father. Her mother should be relatively easy to win over unless she is a single mom. Does her dad hunt? Does he golf? Does he fish? Does he like sports? Is he an avid World War II relic collector? Maybe he just likes John Wayne and James Bond movies.* Whatever things he is interested in, check into them. Watch a John Wayne film or two. (MCCLINTOCK, THE SONS OF KATIE ELDER, RIO LOBO, and RIO BRAVO should suffice.) Google World War II memorabilia and even check out how much money that kind of stuff is going for on eBay. His favorite NFL team is the Saints? Find out some facts, watch some recent footage, and find out when the next game is.

---

*Who doesn't?

WARNING: Don't become the expert. It will annoy her dad if you try to look like you know more than he does. He needs to be the expert, and you just defer to his knowledge. And if he says something you know is wrong, just go with it. Nothing is worse than you accidently making her dad feel stupid because you couldn't keep your mouth shut. Think about how you feel when someone points out a mistake *you've* made. It's hard to come back from that.

If he likes the Lakers and you're not really a fan, don't pretend to be. Be honest! Don't diss them or anything; just be like, "Oh, I can't *believe* you're a Lakers fan! They're good and all, but it's all about the Kings." Say it with a playful smile, and then let him tell you why the Lakers are better. Tell him you'll give them a close second. Don't come over decked out in purple and gold, telling him how you should have been born six feet five inches tall to fulfill the lifelong dream you've had about playing for the Lakers when you just found out who they were. Then you're being fake, and fake is pretty easy to see through. Everyone will wonder what else you're lying about.

Once you have done your homework on her dad (and brothers if she has them), focus on your appearance. First of all, dress nicely. Your old Star Wars t-shirt and jeans with holes in them are not appropriate. Flip flops should stay in the closet. Dress like you did to first impress her. If you're going to her parents' house, wear khaki shorts, a Polo shirt, and boat shoes with a brown belt unless your shirt is untucked. Groom yourself, please. This means minimum facial hair—and for heaven's sake, keep your nails short. You aren't a trannie, so don't act like it. Remember that you should smell nice too. Two to three sprays of cologne and some serious deodorant are a must in this situation. No one like pit stains or B.O.

Once you've got the parent-appropriate look (and smell) going on, head off to buy her and her mother flowers. If you are a regular guy meeting a regular girl's parents, don't go overboard here—just go to the local grocery store and get some. If you are a heart surgeon and her parents are gazillionaires, step up your game and spring for a florist—and have the flowers sent ahead.

When you enter, hug your girlfriend, but don't kiss her in front of your parents. Gross! And don't get all touchy-feely just because you are nervous. They are just now meeting you, and they don't need you to be Mr. Octopus with a thousand hands on the child they've raised since birth and care about more than anything else.

Smile and look her mother in the eye, because that is who you'll be meeting first. Don't be the cheesy weirdo who kisses her mother's hand and asks if she is really her sister because she doesn't look old enough to be her mother. Take your used-car-salesman lines elsewhere.

You can take her mother's hand in both of yours, while looking her in the eye and smiling, and tell her

how nice it is to finally meet her and how much you've been looking forward to it. You can be honest and tell her that you're a little nervous, actually.

When her father comes to shake your hand, do it right. If you don't have a good handshake, then what the hell have you been doing all these years? Thankfully, it's never too late to learn. First, look her father in the eye and offer your hand. Squeeze his firmly and shake no more than twice, but probably just once, then let go. Don't go two-handed here because body language experts say that in men, it makes it seem like you're the one who wants to be in control, which will go over like a ton of bricks. And don't try to crush his bones! You won't win him over if you are later driving him to the orthopedic surgeon because you suddenly became Hulk Hogan during the handshake. Firm and quick with eye contact—it's not rocket science.

Hopefully her father will clap you on the back and start asking questions; but let's face it—not everyone is so outgoing. He might be more like Robert DeNiro in *Meet the Fockers*. The mother will likely be the first to start the conversation, and it could go something like this.

You've already handed her the flowers, so she makes herself busy getting out a vase.

"Mike, these are so nice. You didn't have to do that!" (Yes you did.) Smile when she says it. If you must speak, then say something neutral like "I know, but I wanted to." Keep smiling.

"So Mike, Lucy tells me you are a chemical engineer. Where are you working?"

"Mrs. Kettermen, I work at Allied Chem. It's over on I-95." Smile, smile, smile, but casually lean against the counter or wall like you belong there.

"Oh, that's so nice."

Her dad might jump in at this point. "Say, Billy Haskins used to work over there. Don't know if he's still there. Do you know Billy Haskins, Mike?"

Never lie to them to try to make a good impression unless they ask you if you are sleeping with their daughter. Then say *no*!

Just admit that you don't know Billy Haskins and move on. But here is the thing you need to remember about moving on: they are asking you questions to try to start a conversation because everyone in that room is terrified of the awkward silence. However, this means don't give one-word answers and then shut up. You want to be easy to get to know. This is a fine line. Don't constantly talk about yourself either, or they will think you are a narcissist. This is not the time to tell them about all the awards you've won and how you are the best at everything you've ever tried. Keep talking, but not about yourself.

Ask them questions. Make a list of questions beforehand and study it so you know the kinds of things you can ask. This too is part of the homework. Like the Boy Scouts, be prepared!

"Sorry Mr. Kettermen, that name doesn't ring a bell. I might know Mr. Haskins if I saw him, but I'm kind of new over there. So is he a chemical engineer, too?"

Other ways to keep this conversation going are by asking her father about his work. It's only fair because he asked about yours. Remember that people love to talk about themselves and the things they are passionate about.

"Mr. Kettermen, tell me more about what you do." He might give you a good long answer that allows you to ask more questions. Tell him how interesting his work sounds (even if it isn't).

If her mother works, don't leave her out! Ask her about her teaching job, and then ask her if she has any crazy stories about the kids she's taught. Or perhaps she could tell you all about the strange things she's had to do as a legal secretary. The list goes on.

Say something like, "I can see where Lucy gets her work ethic from!" Compliment their daughter on meaningful things in front of them. Don't compliment her on her beauty or how good her butt looks in those jeans she's wearing. Compliment her mind, her work ethic, or her compassion. Let them know that you have taken time to actually get to know their daughter, and that you are not a big jerk that her dad is going to have to get Sal, the local muscle, to deal with. Keep your kneecaps intact and bring up the fact that you love that Lucy volunteers on Saturdays, and that you've never met anyone with as good of a heart as hers.

When the time comes to talk to her dad one-on-one, because it probably will, you can start by saying, "Lucy tells me you are an avid John Wayne fan."

"That's putting it mildly, son."

"I haven't seen a lot of his films, but I actually ended up watching one the other day called *Big Jake*. Have you seen that one?" Of course he has, greenhorn.

"Have I seen it? I have the Limited Edition Collector's DVD signed by John Wayne's grandson! If you thought that was a good movie, you should check out *Rio Bravo*."

"I've never heard of that one. What's it about?" He will probably suggest you borrow it if he owns it and he likes you. Or he might just tell you to check it out sometime if he doesn't own it or he is still a little uncertain about you.

The premise is the same no matter what his hobby is. Ask him about it and tell him that you don't know that much, but you did see _____ (fill in the blank) recently. Then, let him tell you more about it. It's easy.

If her mom cooks during your get-together, you eat and you love it. If you have food allergies, please let your girlfriend know to let her mother know *before* you arrive—like two or three days before. Otherwise it will be awkward, embarrassing, and the

mother will feel horrible the whole time. You don't want that, just like you don't want her dad to have to stab an epipen in your leg due to your horrendous shellfish allergy.

Maybe you could say something at the end of the meal like, "Mrs. Kettermen, that was so good! I'm not much of a cook, so it won't do me any good to ask you for the recipe, but next time you make that can I invite myself over?" Say it leaning slightly back with both hands on your stomach and a smile on your face. And then drop it. Too many compliments make them seem fake and then it gets awkward. When you're ready to leave, hug her mother with a side hug and shake her father's hand again. Thank them both for dinner and tell her dad you enjoyed seeing his collection of World War II relics or whatever.

Then hug your girlfriend, tell her you will call her later, and say goodnight. Again, no kissing or being touchy in front of her parents, even if she wants to! Show some respect.

If you are eating out at a restaurant, the premise is the same. Compliment the chef of the restaurant they have chosen instead of the mother and tell them that next time, the two of you will be the ones taking them out for dinner. And don't order the most expensive thing on the menu or complain about it once you get your meal. Nothing is more annoying. If your steak isn't perfect or you ordered asparagus WITHOUT almond slivers and they brought the almond slivers, suffer in silence.

And remember, the way you treat the people who are serving you is the way her parents will think you are going to treat their daughter, so make it good. Don't insult them by trying to pay this time or by offering to leave the tip. It's tacky to quibble over such things, especially in public. Again, thank them for dinner and tell them you will be taking them out next time.

Single mothers are a different animal. They are the biggest, baddest mama bears out there. They have had to be the mother *and* the father, so they are used to fiercely protecting their daughters. This might mean they've built up a giant wall that you'd have to be a skilled mountain climber to get over. Or it might not. But if it does, what *that* mother is looking for are these few things:

- **Consistency.** Do you consistently treat her daughter like a queen? Are you always there when she needs you? Do you ever break dates? Do you always make the daughter and mother feel important? Single moms are won over after a period of time.

- **Trustworthiness.** If the mother is divorced, than she has probably been hurt in many ways and is already wary of you because you

are a man. The last thing she wants is for
her daughter to go through what she went
through. Do not give the daughter or mother a
reason *not* to trust you. Be where you say you
are going to be. Call when you are supposed
to (every day if you are at the parent stage).
Don't hang around other women alone unless
you are related.

➤ **Kindness.** Be kind in every way to her
daughter. Be overly thoughtful. Don't be
anything like her deadbeat dad was, and you
will find that she and her mother both will
come to rely on you and expect you to stay in
their lives.

Your Big Relationship Fears

Why is it that the word "man" seems to be synonymous with commitment-phobe? Okay, I know all men aren't like that, but once you are successfully dating, it can be hard to totally give up the fun single life! Let's face it: you love your freedom, and there is nothing wrong with that. If you are still feeling like that, then you just aren't ready for a girlfriend who will tie you down, no matter how great that girl might be, so take a step back.

The worst thing you can do if you are worried about the loss of freedom that a relationship brings is jump into a relationship because you're being pressured to do so. One of you will just end up disappointed, and you'll get a bad reputation among the ladies—especially if you live in a small town.

Also, is if you ever admit to a future girlfriend that you cheated on your former girlfriend, all the trust you've built up will fly out the window the second those words leave your mouth. You might as well tattoo a big scarlet letter on your forehead and walk around like that for the rest of your natural life.

If you think that it won't follow you around for-ever, you're wrong. Just yesterday, I was sitting with my mother and one of her friends having lunch, and a man that I recognized but could not put a name to walked in. He smiled at us and waved. Of course I asked my mother who it was, and she told me his name.

"He's the one who cheated on his wife, Susan. Poor thing."

Her friend leaned over conspiratorially, "You know back in high school he cheated on Lisa too. Everyone tried to warn Susan before she married him. Once a cheater, always a cheater."

I asked how long ago he and Susan had been married. The answer? Twenty years ago. He'd been faithful to his new wife for about eighteen years, but that small fact doesn't matter. Everyone is still talking about Susan and Lisa and what a poor excuse for a man he is. His new wife is from another state and is probably clueless as to what went on, or else she wouldn't be his new wife.

Compromise and co-dependence are two scary things that come with any relationship. Also, let's just be honest, you're going to be having the same sex with the same person for who knows how long.

For so long now, you've been looking out for numero uno. You eat whatever you feel like eating; you watch whatever you want on TV; you drink milk straight from the carton; and you burp and leave beer bottles on the counter because you just feel like it. You don't need to schedule a guy's night—every night is guy's night!

Then *she* comes along. Suddenly, she wants to watch Bravo and go see Katherine Heigl films and drink sugar-free peppermint lattes. That is seriously cutting into your World of Warcraft, beer-drinking time.

All of a sudden, the things you used to do without hesitation have to be cleared with this beautiful life-invader that you are now dating. At first, you don't mind as much because you're excited to get to know her. But after a few weeks of asking if it is okay if you go fishing instead of sitting through a local rendition of the Vagina Monologues, you are missing that make-your-own-rules attitude that you once had back when you were blessedly single. Plus now you have to pretend that you *didn't* notice how big those waitress's boobs were or suffer her wrath!

Here is the thing to remember when you start feeling like her painted red fingernails are slowly closing in around your lungs and that you are suffocating, one chick-flick at a time. You went through a lot to find her, impress her, and impress her loved ones, so at some point you thought she was worth it. Think about the things you like about her. Take a few deep, free breaths and think of fly fishing. And then have a conversation with her.

"Lucy, I love spending time with you. You are one of the best things that has ever happened to me. But I

want to make sure that you always have time to enjoy the things that you love that I might not be as into, and that I have that time too. What if we made every other Saturday afternoon a time when we can do our own thing. I know you don't want to go shoot skeet and drink beer with me and Larry; and even though I love spending time with you, watching you try on shoes in Dillard's isn't that fun for me either. Would you be okay with something like that as long as it is flexible?"

Make sure she knows that you are not leaving her or criticizing her, just that you would like to carve out some time for yourself, and she should too. Unless she is insane, she'll agree to your well-worded plan or some modified version or it.

Once you clear up the "me time" issue, you can tackle the sex issue. She is the way she is in bed. You are probably not dating a porn-star. If you want her to be more adventurous, you need to be more adventurous.

There is an old saying: "If you want more, give more." It's true. I'm going to let you in on a little secret as to why peoples' sex drives dry up. Men are always horny and ready to go, but women are like wind-up toys. You've got to work a little bit to get them going, sexually and otherwise.

Let me give you the best piece of advice you will ever hear in this arena. Ever. **Women need an emotional connection before they want a physical connection.** It is like a math problem.

A + B = C

A—The need of a woman to be held, fussed over, given flowers, and made to laugh	B—You doing all those things before you try to grab her boobs or stick your hand down her pants	C—Her having sex with you

When thinking about this, I always think about the first episode of the show *Nip/Tuck*. It shows the two doctors: one is having sex with his wife, and the other is having sex with a model he just met. The doctor that is married is on top, missionary position. He is thinking about firing the gardener, and she is thinking about her "to do" list while they are boringly rhythmic. The other doctor with the model is having wild, doggie-style sex with the woman screaming. There is no thinking—it's just primal. I get that you don't want to end up like couple number one.

Early in the relationship, you were like rabbits! You were like couple number two and you couldn't keep your hands off of each other. It's because it was new. Later on, or even if you get married, you're lucky

to have sex twice a week, and she lets you know you better be grateful when it does happen!

Trust me on this small piece of advice that I've imparted. Let her know you have needs; BUT in the same breath, let her know that you understand that she has needs too and that they aren't always physical ones like yours. Tell her that you are going to make a real effort to meet those needs, and don't say anything else. She doesn't need you to spell out the rest. Actions speak louder than words; and when you begin acting on it, you should get a result. You scratch her back, and she will scratch yours.

This means that you need to be more thoughtful than anyone she has ever dated. You want sex? She wants you to give her a back massage without having to ask for one. Do that, and then you might get some. She likes shoes, so surprise her with some in her size. Maybe you don't have any money. That's okay. Just do the dishes or clean the house. Draw her a bath and leave her alone until she is done. These are really nice things that she will appreciate.

Maybe she saw a journal she thought was pretty when you were both together days ago. Perhaps it was a pair of earrings. Remember that and bring it to her when you see her next. Don't make a big deal out of it or hold it over her head. Just hand it to her and say, "This is for you. I remembered that you liked it." Or bring her the coffee that she always orders when she goes out to Starbucks. It's the little things that are important to her—like folding her laundry or putting your arm around her on the couch.

Cuddle, cuddle, cuddle. Show her affection, tell her she is beautiful, and tell her that she looks nice as often as you remember to say it. If you see her without her makeup, tell her she is a natural beauty. Make her feel good about herself, and she will make you feel great later.

When you are out, lean over and whisper in her ear, "Every man here is jealous of me because I'm with the most beautiful woman in the room." Doing a culmination of little things like this will get her to the bedroom and just make your lives together generally better.

Once you get there, the battle is eighty-five percent over. If you are getting bored with the same position over and over, do your research! Google different sexual positions or buy a book on Amazon and have it shipped to your house discreetly. When you are in the bedroom,* suggest whatever it is that you want to try. She will most likely try it if you suggest it. If you are adventurous, she will follow along. Even better, don't suggest it. Just pick her up and do it. That is sure to bring out something primal, and primal is good.

In saying that, if you're into toys in the bedroom, you might want to have a conversation about THAT before you go into the bedroom—and be prepared for

---

*Or living room floor, wherever!

her to be incredibly uncomfortable. It may take some time before she is ready to try anything like that. The most important thing is that you make her feel safe and comfortable. So if she says to stop, don't keep pounding away because you will make her feel dirty and worthless. If you disregard her need in this, you will do irreparable damage to your relationship, so tread carefully in this area.

For more about the sex life in a long-term relationship, see the marriage chapters.

You've Found "The One." Now What?

Once you realize that you've found the woman you want to spend the rest of your life with and be the mother of your children, what are you supposed to do now? Date for the next ten years? Think again.

I promise you this: after a year of dating, if you haven't brought up marriage, she's going to start hinting about it. It might even happen sooner than that. If you ignore it or tell her you aren't ready, all she hears is that you are waiting for someone better to come along. Before too long, she will be headed for greener pastures, and you'll be starting over because you were too chicken to broach the "M" word.

First of all, unless she has discussed this with you previously and expressed that she wants to do this, don't ask her to move in with you. All she really wants at this point is to get married or else she wouldn't still be with you, so asking her to move in is a slap in the face. She will be embarrassed to tell her family and embarrassed to face yours unless her family isn't in the picture.

When you realize that things are great and she is the one, the first thing to do BEFORE you pop the question is start saving money. Seriously—you are really going to need it. And I'm not talking about saving a few hundred bucks. I'm talking about a few thousand. Among other things I do, I moonlight as a wedding coordinator, so I'm going to break down the cost of things for you in this book.

Why so much? Your first expense is going to be the engagement ring. This should cost you two month's salary. Popping the question shouldn't come out of nowhere. You should have discussed marriage at this point so you don't deal with rejection. Have you thought about the cost of renting an apartment or a down payment on a house? How about the cost of a wedding if her family doesn't help out? Did you know your family pays for the rehearsal dinner?

Once you are financially ready to pop the big question, you can do one of three things. First, you could find out her ring size and go out and choose a ring for her that you like. In my opinion, unless she tells you she wants to be surprised, this is the dumbest idea ever. More than likely, she has been perusing wedding magazines and jewelry stores since she was a little girl. She already knows what kind of ring she wants, and she is the one who will be wearing it for the rest of her life, not you! People are going to be asking to see it once you are engaged multiple times a day. You want her to thrust her hand out to them with pride, not shyly look down and reluctantly hold her hand out, embarrassed. When my former husband and I were talking about getting married, he told me that he wanted to pick out my ring. I have VERY particular tastes, and I immediately told him that it was a bad idea. He asked me why it was a bad idea, so I said, "Let's play a game. Get online and show me what you would pick out for me."

We went to a few websites, and he picked out seven or eight horrendous rings that I wouldn't be caught dead in. Personally, I truly dislike pear-shaped diamond, and I didn't want anything that actually stuck up on top of the ring or was held on with prongs. I'm too clumsy and would probably lose the diamond. He was baffled that I didn't like what he had chosen. He then asked me what I did like.

"That's easy!" I said. I went to my purse, pulled out my wallet, and showed him a picture of a ring that I had found in a magazine three years prior to meeting him and had carried with me ever since.

His response was, "This looks nothing like what I would have gotten you." I told him I knew it didn't, and I would have been disappointed with what he had chosen, even if I hadn't said so.*

---

*With my personality, I would have said so.

Your second option is the more traditional one. Take her ring shopping yourself. It will be exciting! Tell her how much you have saved and kindly ask her to try to stay in that price range. She will be excited that you've thought far enough ahead to save for this day. However, don't buy it in front of her. Save the dirty work for later when she isn't there. Some places offer payment plans, so be sure to check into that.

Your third option is to have a friend ask her to go looking at rings for fun. Get the friend to take pictures of "the one" on her camera phone and report back to you. Then you can totally surprise her, but still get her what she wants. Everyone wins!

If you are lucky enough to have a family heirloom ring that you would like to give her, show it to her first and ask her if she might like to have the diamonds reset in a more contemporary setting. She might like it just the way it is, and that is great for your wallet!

Remember, she will be buying you a ring too. So after you ask for her hand in marriage, tell her what kind of band you would like as well as your ring size. You can get fitted at the jewelry store where you buy her ring and check out the different styles they offer for men too.

Once you are ready to ask her to marry you, I beg you—even if you don't have a romantic bone in your body and you sweat Gatorade, make it special! If you don't know how, ask a female friend or family member for help. One thing to remember is to make it a surprise!

When my former husband proposed to me, I had no idea that it was happening when it did. We had discussed it and tried on rings. He even asked me what was important to me in a proposal. I'm a very family-oriented person, so I told him it would be special to me if my family were to be there when it happened, especially my sister.

My sister lives in a different town; and at the time, she was a waitress. My boyfriend asked for my parents' help, and they told us they were going to visit my sister that week and asked if we could come. We all rode together, and my boyfriend had given the ring to my mother before we got in the car. When we got to the restaurant where my sister worked and were seated, my mother excused herself to go to the restroom and handed off the ring to my sister. At the end of the meal, a different waitress came by and brought us a piece of cake but kept standing at our table. Then, a waiter came by and put some caramel sauce on top of the cake and stood next to the waitress. Then another waitress came out and spooned some whipped cream onto our cake and stood next to the waiter. Another waitress came out with a cherry, which she placed on top of the dessert. The whole time, I was thinking, "*Whose birthday is it?*" Finally, my sister came out holding the ring box, and my former husband got down on one knee in front of the whole restaurant and asked me to marry him.

Knowing he had already asked my father's permission, I said yes! It was so special that he made my family, especially my sister, part of such an important day.

Maybe your girlfriend isn't close with her family, or maybe she wants your moment to be private. These are all things that you can easily work with.

If she has a penchant for being a bit dramatic and loves attention (in a good way), then let several of her closest friends and family in on the secret. Take her out to dinner and then have each of them walk in at the end of the meal carrying a single flower, which they hand to her. Once the last one, a family member, hands her the final flower, be on your knee with the ring in your hand.

Go to the movies. At the end of the film, have the manager project, "Will You Marry Me, Lucy?" on the screen. This might be funny if there is more than one Lucy there, but it will be amazing for you.

Go to a professional baseball game and have them put that same message on their big screen during half-time.

Maybe she has a favorite talk show. Call in and ask if you can propose to her on the show.

If she is a more private person, take her to the scene of your first date, give her flowers, and ask her there.

Whatever it is that you decide to do, it needs to be a story she can tell her family, friends, and later on your children and grandchildren. Make it a wonderful memory.

I asked my grandmother once how my grandfather proposed, and she told me that they had gone to the drive-in movie theater on their first date, so he took her back to the drive-in and proposed there. She said he was so thoughtful, and I loved hearing her story.

When I asked my mother how my father proposed, she said, "He really didn't. One day we were sitting on the couch, and he just said, 'Let's get married,' and I agreed. Your dad hasn't ever been accused of being romantic!"

Don't let THAT be the story she tells everyone.

So what are the other things you need to start saving money for? The honeymoon, the rehearsal dinner (if your family won't be chipping in), groomsmen gifts, gifts for your parents and in-laws, a tuxedo, and of course, a down payment for a new house if you are both moving out of your apartments or parents' homes. If you are doing the apartment thing first, you'll need to remember that you'll have to pay a deposit probably equal to the first month's rent along with the first month's rent. Getting married is expensive!

The honeymoon that I took for five days to Kauai was amazing and incredibly memorable. When looking to book it online through one of the travel websites, it

cost six thousand dollars! We weren't flying first class or staying in the most expensive hotel, either! Travel is just expensive!

While moaning and groaning about the cost of this to my dad over dinner one night, he suggested that I tell my then-fiancé to go and see a travel agent. My first thought was, "*Oh, great, another expense. At this rate, we'll never get married!*"

As it turns out, travel agents don't charge for their services. They get paid by the companies they represent, and they get much better deals on things than you or I will ever get! We went to our travel agent's office with extremely low expectations and a print-out of the honeymoon we wanted to take.

Our travel agent, Lynne, took a look at the travel website's price, and laughed! "Oh my," she said, "that sure is pricey."

With a few strokes of her keyboard and a big grin, she handed us a brochure of the island of Kauai and asked if we had considered any activities while we were there along with our hotel, airfare, and car rental.

I was the voice of reason. "I don't think we can afford it."

She said, "I think you can!" She handed us another printout with the hotel we wanted to stay in, two plane tickets, a rental car, and a few activities included. The only difference was we got more than we wanted for three thousand dollars less! That's right—fifty percent off the website's "best" price. Travel agents are the way to go!

Next on your list is the rehearsal dinner. Traditionally, your parents pay for this, and the bride's parents pay for the wedding. My ex-husband's family is from another country. Not only could they not get visas to come, but they didn't pay for anything, leaving him to pay for it.

Let's be honest: we are not all millionaires. It would be nice if that were the case! Don't feel like it has to be a black-tie affair, especially if your family is not in a position to do this for you. Express to your future bride that you would like to keep the number small and intimate, meaning just immediate family and the wedding party.

You can have the dinner at someone's house if you are on an extremely tight budget, and you can ask a family member or a few friends of the family to help out with the food. You will need to rent tables and table cloths as well as restaurant plates, cutlery, and cloth napkins if you go the more formal route. I'm from Louisiana, and people have informal rehearsal dinners all the time. They might have a crawfish boil or a big pot of gumbo, and everyone wears jeans. This gives everyone the ability to relax and get to know each other.

Another option is finding a local restaurant or renting the event room at your church. Restaurants usually have packages put together for these sorts of

events, so you will just need to let them know your price range, and they will do the rest.

You may want to talk to your bride-to-be about making a slide show to make the evening special once you have the venue down.

Then you will need to get a gift for your groomsmen and parents as well as your future in-laws. The bride may take care of the gifts for her parents, or she may expect your help, so be willing.

For your groomsmen, get them a pair of cufflinks that they can wear on the big day, or a money clip with your wedding date engraved. These can be inexpensive items that will be nice enough to give as gifts on the special occasion. Check online for deals on these items so you aren't paying what you would pay at a gentlemen's store. Ask your bride to wrap them so they look great when you actually hand them over.

Your father might also receive these cufflinks, and you can find a nice pair of earrings or a pearl bracelet for your mother. I personally gave my father a gift certificate for a massage after the entire headache he went through with the wedding, and I ordered my mother a crystal vase from Tiffany and Co. Each gift cost about seventy dollars. My husband sent his mother a pearl bracelet and earrings. Tickets to the next big football game might be nice for dear old Dad too!

Finally, get your bride a gift. It doesn't have to be big, but it has to be thoughtful. Reassure her that she is making the right decision by writing her a letter about how much she means to you and how you aren't nervous at all. If you aren't creative, use this template.

Dear Lucy,

I am the luckiest man alive. I feel like my life started when I met you. Until the day we met in Starbucks, I didn't know what was missing from my life; but now, having you in my life is like breathing. You are the missing piece of the puzzle, and now my life feels perfect.

Most guys might be a little nervous about tying the knot, but I'm not nervous at all. The jittery feeling in the pit of my stomach is pure excitement. I can't wait to see you dressed up in your beautiful wedding dress, walking toward me. You'll be the most beautiful woman in the room tomorrow and always.

I know that one day, we are going to have children together, and someday we will grow old together and tell our grandchildren about this day—the day it all began. Thank you so much for saying yes to me, to us. I love everything about you, even the way you snore, even though you think you don't! I love you, Lucy.

See you down the aisle! I'll be the one smiling like I just won the lottery.

Love,

Mike

She will pull out this letter from time to time for the rest of her life and smile when she thinks about how amazing you are. She will know that really, she is the lucky one. Women want a man who makes them feel like a woman in a Nicholas Sparks novel.

Other than that, keep your mouth shut and let her plan the day she has been planning since she was four. Bottom Line: just do what she says and show up when she asks you. Oh, and be on time. You can play nine holes of golf later.

The next big expense is saving for a house. Usually if you are a first-time home buyer, you can get all kinds of great deals like zero percent or three percent down, which is amazing. The important thing here is to save like there is no tomorrow and realize that you are just not going to get everything you want. My ex-husband and I had to put ten thousand dollars down and pay closing costs as well as a realtor fee. We lived in a place where real estate hadn't sky-rocketed. Keep all of this in mind. Remind your wife or girlfriend that even though she wants those shoes or she wants to eat out, you will be eating in your new house soon enough, so keep the bigger picture in mind!

The Honeymoon is Over

Marriage is work. It's harder than that construction job you had one summer—the one where you worked in the hot sun all day long and had to lift things heavier than you. Don't let anyone convince you otherwise because they are lying! This can be scarier than dating because it is nothing like the twenty-second "happily-ever-after" clip at the end of a movie when they are all smiles or dancing around like little airplanes. This is real, no-sex-until-you-take-out-the-trash, life.

Everyone is going to tell you when you get married that there are two words that are the secret to a successful marriage, and they are: "Yes, dear."

The woman in me wants to tell you that it is TRUE! But let's be honest, there are going to be times when she is wrong. No one is right all of the time.* For whatever reason you are disagreeing, think about how you feel when you are called out for being wrong and don't make her feel small. Really listen to what she is saying because what if she has something valid to say? Just

---

*Except for me.

remember: when you disagree on something, the most important thing is to fight fair—no sucker punches.

That means that no one throws around the d-word unless you are really, REALLY ready to actually walk away from your marriage forever.

You will find that in marriage, you have the same fights over and over again. That might sound ridiculous, but it is true. You will find yourselves fighting about one thing: and somehow, by the end of the argument, you're fighting about something totally different! Now, instead of arguing about who is going to do the dishes, you are arguing about your sex life or lack thereof! How did that happen?

Let me let you in on a secret: she is going to bring up the past. It's how women fight. So you will too, just to have a dog in the fight; and finally after some hurtful words, you'll get around to your real main issue. It seems to just be the way things work because women are incapable of not bringing up what you've done wrong before.

For my ex and me, it always seemed to come down to sex. I would think we were fighting because I didn't do the dishes, and it turns out we were really fighting because he thought we weren't having sex enough.

Here's the deal: on your honeymoon, you had sex every day! She was on fire, wearing sexy little black numbers with not much left to the imagination. Those were the good ol' days!

Now, if you're lucky, once or twice a week she will look at you, and you will wiggle your eyebrows and smile. She will sigh, look down at her holey t-shirt and sweatpants, and shrug her shoulders to indicate that yes, she will deign to sleep with you tonight, but ONLY if it's the missionary position, and only if you take a shower first. She will hurry out of her grannie panties and jump under the covers, and the whole process will be done in minutes. Then, she'll just go about business as usual, safe for a few more days.

I cannot tell you how many times I've heard my friends talking about how they have to hurry up and get some clothes on as soon as they get out of the shower so their husbands don't get any "ideas." It's true.

Why? What changed? First off, sex for you is like breathing. You can get it up almost any time, and almost everything you see turns you on. That's truly wonderful for you, dude. But for women, the things that turn us on are a little different.

You are a match. All it takes is one little strike against the matchbox, and you are lit up like Christmas. Women are like old-school flint. You need steel, you need flint, and the conditions better be perfect to get a flame. After about one hundred strikes, the fire is going to finally ignite. Then you need to protect that flame and blow on it and all that other Boy Scout stuff, or it will go out.

It's the same principle with men and women. Seriously! You can see a hot girl on TV, and you are ready to grab your wife, throw her down on the kitchen floor, and go! She bends over and you catch a little cleavage, and it's on because you are still attracted to the hot woman you married!

Don't worry; just because she doesn't show it like you do, she is still attracted to you too. Why? This is because women usually don't marry for looks. She fell in love with the you on the inside. If you treat her right, even if you gain forty pounds and go totally bald, she is going to stay with you because she genuinely loves you. Don't let her lack of sex drive make you think she has lost attraction to you. I have guy friends who have told me in confidence that when the sex started losing its appeal, they started to diet and hit the gym so their girlfriends or wives would be more attracted to them. I told each of them that I promised that it wasn't because of that. If you want to go to the gym for yourself, that's awesome! More power to you! If you are pumping iron to make your sex life better, step away from the leg press machine and get home. She will automatically think that you are trying to tell *her* that she needs to get to the gym, which will make her feel even less sexy. You will be taking more time away from her too, when what she really needs is for you to fall in love with her all over again.

Take the time to do something romantic, even if it's the smallest thing, every few days. A Facebook friend of mine just posted a picture of her husband holding flowers. The caption read, "Ryan is the best husband ever. He went to the store for milk and eggs, and he came back with Friday Flowers. I love Friday Flowers and I love Ryan!" This small gesture made him look like a king in front of everyone she knows, and it made her very happy. It will make him happy later.

My ex-husband is Latin, and they are ridiculously passionate. He married me, and I'm just not affectionate or touchy-feely in any way—in public especially—so he always got his feelings hurt because I wasn't expressing my love for him like he thought I should. Here is the important thing: find out how you each show affection to the other. With me, I like to cook to show love. It's time consuming, but the result is usually pretty good and I like to see another person satisfied. He liked to show love by trying to touch me or hold me, and he didn't understand why I didn't do exactly the same thing. We love like we want to be loved.

I say that to tell you that you need to find out how your wife wants affection if you want sex. **Earlier, I said that women need an emotional connection before they can have a physical one.** This is so true!

I was always at work before my ex-husband and son ever woke up. When I came home after being on my feet all day, I was constantly watching to make sure my son didn't stick cereal in his ears while I was *still* on my feet making dinner. Then I tried to clean up and

finally sit down for the first time since six a.m. to eat. He would come in, eat, and turn on the Outdoor Channel. While he did that, I put our son to bed, put a load of laundry in, and picked up toys. He would wander into the kitchen and, while I was unloading the dishwasher and thinking about how much I need to pee, he would reach out with his hand and honk my boob and wriggle his eyebrows like I should be incredibly turned on.

Honestly? I was already resentful that his ass had been sitting around on the couch all day and that I'm picking up after him more than I'm picking up after my two year old—and when was the last time he made dinner?

His honking my boob made me want to knee him in the balls, step over him, and continue with the stuff that won't get done unless I do it—like making sure everyone has clothes to wear the next day.

You may have experienced a similar situation. One time, I turned around and honked him in the nuts and asked him if he liked that. He got so mad he wouldn't talk to me for the rest of the evening. No one actually likes that! That is *not* what women want.

Wives are not your blow up dolls. We are people who don't want to be treated like we are honking toys. The fact that guys don't seem to know this baffles me. Random grabbing doesn't make us feel sexy or good about ourselves. It makes us feel like you are inept cavemen who can't control your hand functions.

Okay, enough of my soapbox. Here is what this boils down to: Women's sex drives are affected by our stress levels, how tired we are, and how mad we are at you.

These are some ways to breathe some life back into your bedroom.

Make arrangements to pick up your children for a change.

If you don't have kids yet, skip to the next one. If you do have children, ask your parents or her parents for some help if you can't get off work thirty minutes early. Call her and tell her not to worry, that you've got the kids taken care of, and she should just relax and go home to watch that Real Housewives episode that has been on the DVR for three months. Tell her you're doing this because she deserves a little break. Don't express why you're doing it, and don't expect her to jump on top of you like a spider monkey the minute you walk through the door. She might; but depending on how bad it is, she may need several days of thoughtfulness before she realizes that she needs to be thoughtful too. If you go to kiss her hello and she gives you a peck in response with the "mwuah" sound, she isn't ready.

Deal with dinner.

Even though she is trying to be a good wife, this is not the 1950s, so she does not have to be June Cleaver every night of the week. Vacuuming in pearls? Get real.

Vacuuming in dirty sweat pants with applesauce on them is far more likely. Before she leaves for work, let her know that you have dinner taken care of tonight. Whether you cook a full meal or just pick up dinner from her favorite restaurant, make it special by setting the table. Don't you dare let her get up to get herself a refill or touch a dish, even if she insists. Instead, run a bath for her and tell her to relax and read a magazine while you take care of the dishes. Trust me; this will go A LONG WAY!

Give her a massage.

If she has had a tough day, tell her to sit down and that you will take over. If that means doing the laundry or taking care of the kids for a few minutes, then so be it. After a little while, have her lie down and give her a real massage for longer than two minutes. And please, PLEASE don't say, "My turn!" It ruins the relaxed mood you just created by putting back all the tension you just helped her release. It will just be another thing she can't enjoy because she has something else to do. Your massage can wait. I'm not saying you can't have one too, but don't choose that moment to demand quid pro quo.

Act like you are dating.

Things were fun when you were dating because YOU still made an effort back then, and so did she. It wasn't all about TV, parent/teacher conferences, and soccer games. Hire a babysitter and surprise your wife with one of the dates from the dating chapter, or even just dinner out somewhere you both love. Pick up the kids, put them to bed, and tell your wife the laundry can wait. Take her hand, guide her to the bedroom, close and lock the door, and tell her how beautiful she is tonight.

"You are still the most beautiful woman in the room, no matter where we go. I was so proud to be with you tonight."

She will smile, and you will lean in, run your fingers through her hair, and kiss her like you mean it. Let her take the lead, and hopefully she will lead you to the bed where you can have a little (or a lot of) fun.

Clean the whole house.
This includes the stuff you think is "her responsibility." Guess what? It's your responsibility too. How many times has she cleaned up after you? And the kids? And herself and the three dogs? When she gets home, kiss her and tell her how great she is. She will let you know how great you are too! (Just don't do her laundry. This usually has disastrous results.)

Give her a girl's night every now and then.
You survived without her for years. You can do it again for one night a month. Tell her that you think

she should have a girl's night, and that you'll take care of stuff at home. When she goes out, take a deep breath and put away your cell phone. Don't call her to ask how to change a diaper (you know how!), where the kids' snacks and pajamas are, or where she is and what she is doing.

Think about how annoying it is when you are hunting or drinking beer with the guys when she calls to ask where you are or what is taking so you long. It's the same principle. You said you were going to give her some girl time, so give it to her! Unless someone breaks an arm, leave her alone and you will see her when she gets back. If you really need some backup, call your mother or hers.

When she gets back, if you are pouting on the couch because she took forever, you've canceled out all the good you did. Have a smile on your face and ask her if she had a good time. Tell her you are SO glad she finally got some time to herself, because she deserved it.

Take her shopping.

This can be done in many ways. You don't have to, but you can go to the mall with her and stand around bored while she tries on tops that all look the same to you. Tell her to go out and spend $200 on herself (or whatever it is that you can afford). Or sit with her while she shops online. Or don't! Just give her permission to do it. Tell her that you were thinking that she doesn't do enough for herself, and that she should every now and then. (I don't care if you don't agree with this statement; just say it. She will oooh and aaahhh and think you are wonderful.) And if you set a $200 limit, don't fuss at her if she spends $220. If she spends $300, then you are totally justified in saying, "Honey, I said $200, and now we can't buy groceries. I need you to find somewhere to save this month because you really went over our budget."

If it was just a few dollars, seriously, don't be a miser. Those extra twenty dollars will buy you a lot of sex-life miles.

Make sure she is really satisfied.

As a man, you climax pretty much every time you have sex. Whoop-tee-doo. Many women don't have that luxury. If you think I'm lying, Google "How to have an orgasm," or "I've never had an orgasm." There is medication, and there are books, websites, and even exercises to better help women get to that special moment. So think about how much it sucks for her if you come, and she is inches away from coming, but you just roll over and smile at her while she is laying there resenting you again.

How do you remedy this? Use your hands, your mouth, and your tongue. Make sure she comes before you do. It might take a little while; but the more you

practice, the easier it will get, and the more she will want to have sex because she knows she will get something out of it.

If she doesn't want to have sex a lot, you can bet she isn't really getting what she needs, even though she's pretending she is.

Don't get discouraged.

Let's face it, you don't want pity sex! You want her to want you. Don't try to guilt her into having sex with you, because that turns sex into an obligation, which never has good results. Here is the thing I found with my ex-husband: he thought that just because he did one of these things one time, I should be eternally grateful and that the shop should always be open. It doesn't always work like that.

Try doing these things three times a week and see what happens. If it's not working, then let her know that you are making a big effort to make things easier for her, and you are hoping that she will want to spend some intimate time with you as a result. Be honest with her too.

My ex-husband once told me that he would like to see me in some lingerie again every once in a while. I didn't realize that it was as big of a deal as it was to him. I didn't want to put on lingerie. I had just had a child and was fatter than I was when we first got married; so when I saw myself in lingerie, I didn't feel sexy. Once he let me know that didn't matter to him if I had stretch marks, that he just wanted me to make the effort, I went out and bought lingerie and put it on for him. I appreciated his honesty, and I would have never known that my sweatpants were actually an issue for him unless he had told me.

If you are honest with her, and you are consistent in your efforts, there is going to be a positive change. If you start talking, she might tell you something specific that she wants you to do, and you can do that instead of trying all of the things I've listed. Likely though, making this effort consistently will be more than enough.

Don't screw it up.

So you've done some or all of the things on this list, and then you make one little mistake. You said one stupid thing or one mean thing. Guess what, buddy? You just canceled out everything you did. Apologize for being human and start over. Just remember: if you are constantly apologizing, your "sorry" loses its value. Show her you really can stop being insensitive or hurtful, and things will get so much better.

It's the little things that make a big impact. I was looking on Facebook the other day, and I saw that one

of my friends had posted a picture of a bottle of water on her page. Her status read, "Look how wonderful my husband is! He left this for me to find on my running route." The things you are doing don't need to be expensive. You just have to show her you care.

Don't Be *That* Guy

One thing I've learned through dating, marriage, and dating again is that there are some completely clueless men out there who are probably the nicest men in the right situations. An attractive, self-respecting woman isn't going to give them the time of day though, because they say or do stupid things, possibly even to try to "impress" their intended targets.

Not long ago, I was at the bar of my favorite restaurant with some friends, and a young, attractive guy came up to me with a smile on his face, making good eye contact. I have to admit, I turned my body toward him, ready to hear whatever he was going to say. There were a lot of ways he could have gone

- Can I buy you a drink?

- Excuse me, but I couldn't help but notice you from across the room, and I had to come and say hi.

- You're beautiful.

- I'm Dave.

No, he didn't go with any of those simple things. Instead, he went with this: "So, do you like to play the meat flute?"

My reaction was, "Wow. That's what you went with?" And I turned back around and talked to my friends, ignoring him. My friend that heard him rolled her eyes and said, "Oh my gosh! Did he really just say that? What an idiot." He had effectively ruined his chances with me, my gorgeous friend, and any other woman who heard him say that.

The approach is so important. Treat her like a 1940s movie star, and you're probably safe. Be a gentleman. I was in New Orleans recently, and this man who had clearly been enjoying the intoxications of the city came up to my friend and I and slurred out, "Hi, I'm Bryyyyce … .you're kind of cute. And sooooo is your friend," he spit on me, and eyeballed both my friend and me. "Let's go in here, and I'll buy you both a drink."

Don't be so drunk that you can barely stand. That's not attractive, and whatever "beauty" you pull in this state might be someone you are rethinking in the morning. "I thought you said your name was Ellen."

"It's Gerald."

That is the stuff nightmares and *The Hangover* movie is made of. Also, don't hit on a girl AND her friend, especially at the same time!!!

With that said, I want to relay something that happened very recently. One of my best friends in the whole world began dating this guy, and no one could stand him because he made a lot of mistakes. He was the kind of man that feels insecurities and bought into the idea that he needed to make my friend insecure in order to date her. On one of their early dates, he told her she was pretty, but she could stand to lose twenty pounds. Then he would "accidentally" send her text messages he was sending to other women. He really thought this would make her want him more; and let me be honest—it did for a hot minute.

It was very negative attention that he was getting, so everything they ever had together had a dark cloud over it. She doesn't think of him fondly. All she wants from him now is for him to know she is better than he leads her to believe he thinks she is. In addition, he flirted heavily with all of her friends.

This is a pretty big rule of dating: don't hit on your target's friends. In a first encounter, it is confusing and a girl doesn't want to make her friend mad, so she isn't going to go near you. Anything beyond a first encounter, just know that hitting on her friend is a one-way ticket to the curb.

Being *that* guy is a like being Stiffler from *American Pie* … you'll never get women. You don't want to get a reputation for being a douchebag. There are a lot of ways that this guy could have made things work.

Instead of putting her down, he could have tried to make her feel good about herself. If he really thought she needed to lose weight, he could have started suggesting activities they could do together that were more active. He could have told her things like, "When I'm with you, I'm blown away by your smile," instead of creating something negative.

Sending the text messages intended for other women is unacceptable. It sends the message that you are not trustworthy and you don't value her enough to send the right text. It also makes her wonder why she isn't good enough since you are dating other people. If you really are dating other people, it's going to bring forth the "exclusivity" conversation, so be prepared and know what you really want.

Again, don't ever hit on her friends. Not ever. Not even a little bit. That is a train wreck, and the conductor jumped overboard twenty miles back. Instead, treat her friends with respect but keep your distance.

So here's what you need to know: in order to attract women, you have to be confident yourself. Women can smell weakness a mile away. Once you're confident, find a look that will attract women.

When you're ready to settle down into a committed relationship, take note of what's important, then set out to find her. Once your find that special someone, get to know each other and don't change who you are to please her.

When the time comes to settle down with her, be prepared financially and emotionally—those are big decisions that should not be taken lightly. Lastly, always treat her like a Queen, and she'll treat you like her King. You'll both have your needs met, and you'll both be happy. After all, that's what all men and women want—to be happy.

For better or worse, these are the things that women want, and now you know how to give it to them.

Whether you are a single man, dating, or married, I hope this book has helped you. These are the basics of hooking up, getting more serious, or keeping your wife happy! If you have questions beyond this book, you can email me at datingso lutions4U@gmail.com or check out my website: www.datingsolutions4U.webs.com.

Epilogue
The One-Night Stand

This is a controversial topic that I hesitate to address. I'd hate for my mother to die of embarrassment when she reads this, but enough men have asked me about it that I decided to include this chapter. I will say this upfront: one-night stands are not very fulfilling. They're a bit like eating three Pringles when you are starving to death, so read at your own risk! These are some methods that I have had friends tell me about that WORKED.

If you've decided that you are in that phase in your life where you just want a little fun, then you don't want to be the only single schmuck going home alone from the bar...again. There are books out there that would tell you to be rude to the object of your attentions and tell you to put her down or give her back-handed compliments to make her want to please you. In reality, this may work for a short time; but in the long run, you will either get your ass kicked by her body-building friend or her father, or she will turn into a pyscho-maniacal, stage-five clinger, and you'll regret your decisions.

When going in for the kill of a one-night stand, things are considerably easier as long as you aren't too nice. Don't mistake my meaning, though. **Do not be a jerk**—just be jaded. One compliment for the night is enough. If you shower her with compliments or go out of your way to make her comfortable, she is going to think you are either too nice or you are boyfriend material. You don't want to be boyfriend material if you just want a wham-bam-thank-you-ma'am.

This sprint is an easier sell because we are setting you up for one night, not long term. Even though it is short term, there are things you need to invest in. With a one-night stand, mystery is always a good thing. Just like you aren't going to want to know her life story, she doesn't need to know yours. She might ask you lots of questions if she is nervous or if she is looking for a boyfriend. If she is nervous, you will know because she will be touching her hair or her face a lot and will laugh unnecessarily at almost everything you say. You can work with nervous. If she is asking you questions like she is interviewing you for a job, cut and run. One-night stands are shallow. You like the way she looks, she thinks you look okay too, and you go home together.

When you are going out for the night, make sure if you are planning on taking someone home that your house is relatively clean. Don't have dirty dishes piled up in the sink; have clean sheets; your laundry should at least be shoved into your closet; and for heaven's sake, clean your bathroom. She should be thinking about how hot you are in bed, not about whether or not she needs a tetanus shot.

Once you have done all of these things, call a wingman that is going to meet you at the bar. You need a wingman so you don't seem like a weirdo, especially in the beginning. There are a few men who can carry off being alone, but you probably aren't one of them yet.

You and your buddy should not ride together. When you and your lady walk out of the bar rearing to go, it will be a big mood-killer if you have to drop off your friend first. This will give her time to focus on another man, your friend, and time to reconsider jumping into bed with you. Plus, your friend might say something idiotic about you. It's like pouring water on the campfire.

Once you arrive at your destination, make an entrance. Don't walk in with a group of people, but be slightly ahead of your wingman. You want the ladies to see you come in. When you do, don't look around like you're looking for someone. People will think that you're meeting your girlfriend, and then they'll give up on you before you even get started.

This is a good time to remind yourself of all the things you are good at, or at the very least pretend that you've

just beat out Channing Tatum for the Sexiest Man Alive contest. Your entrance should have confidence because we women can smell insecurity from a mile away.

Find an empty seat at the bar for you and your friend and order a beer. Heavy drinking on this outing is prohibited. If you get drunk and slur your speech, every woman you come across, (with the exception of that fifty-year-old coke addict), is going to write you off. You'll start thinking that it's okay to say stupid things and put your hands where they don't belong. You will end up with an ass-kicking from messing with the wrong chick or crabs and an empty wallet from the coke addict.

After you order a drink, put yourself in a position to see the women there and pick a target. Be realistic. You're an amateur, so you probably aren't going home with Adriana Lima tonight. Find someone who is sexy and attractive. Start at a seven, not a ten. Once you are more practiced, then you can go for the ten.

The first thing you should do is catch her eye and hold it for a second. Give her a half-smile or lift one corner of your mouth up, but don't show any teeth. Who do you think you are, Chuckles the Clown? Then look back at your buddy like it was nothing. Don't look at her again for at least five minutes—ten if you can hold out longer. Have your wingman watch her to see if she looks your way again. If she does, after a short time has passed, look at her again.

Repeat what you did the first time. You can even add in a wink, but only if you can do that without looking insane. Practice in the mirror and don't squint too hard. If you are unsure, stick with the eye-contact and half smile.

If she smiles at you this time, go to the bathroom, but make sure she sees you going. If possible, pass her on the way, but don't look at her while you do it. You don't want her to think you want her to follow you there, because you don't. It would be uncomfortable for both of you if she actually did have sex with you there, and she wants more respect than that, even for a one-night stand. Plus you could probably catch hepatitis B from a nasty bar bathroom.

This is what your wingman is here for. He should be watching her for you now. If she watches you go, or even better, goes to the bathroom herself, she is interested in you. If you happen to bump into her back there, you can casually say hi and offer to buy her a drink, but don't be so polite about it. Don't say, "Can I buy you a drink?" Say, "Buy you a drink?" And again, don't smile; just keep a steady eye contact with her.

If she doesn't bump into you back there, she might have come up to the bar close to where you are sitting. Offer her the drink. If neither of these things has happened, come back and ask your friend what happened while you were gone. If she watched you, ask

the bartender to send her a drink. If she is with one other girl, send them both one because it doesn't hurt to butter up her friend so that she is all for the woman you are after going home with you.

When she gets it, lift your beer bottle to her in a toast, and keep talking to your buddy. Ideally, you want her to walk over to you to thank you for the drink, and then you start making small talk. If she doesn't come over to you after the drink, she's either too shy or you've misread the signals. If she keeps making eye contact with you after the drink, it's because she is shy.

If she's too shy, you can still get her home, but there are some things you should consider first. Shy women don't have a lot of experience with men, and they are usually serial monogamists. This is the kind of woman who is looking for Prince Charming on a white horse to sweep her off of her feet. All night she will be thinking with an angel on one shoulder and a devil on the other. The devil will tell her to go for it and screw the consequences, and the angel will want reassurance that you are really a good guy and that you aren't looking for a one-night stand.

I had a friend named Joey once tell me that this girl is what he calls a three-dater. To bag this sweet girl, he says you take her on a series of three dates: coffee and don't kiss her, dinner and kiss her once at her door then leave, and a movie. Then you go to her house and get it on. She is not your one-night-stander, so you are best off moving on unless you plan to invest at least three dates—and hey, at three dates, you might realize you actually like her ... but back to the one-night stand.

If she isn't shy and comes over to thank you for the drink, make small talk for a few minutes. If you are introducing yourself for the first time, do so while looking in her eyes. Even when you take a swig of your beer, look at her. She will smile, and if she is nervous, she will giggle. If she finds herself touching your arm, this is a good sign. Lean in to talk to her so she can smell your cologne. Then, make your move.

This is how your conversation should go down:

You: Want to get outta here?

Her: I guess. Where do you want to go?

You: Let's get a cup of coffee. I'll drive.

If she rode with her friend, that should be fine. If not, encourage her to let your buddy drop her friend off—he might get lucky too. As a last resort, you can drop her friend off, but you run the risk of her changing her mind.

Her: Where do you want to get coffee?

You: My place. I make the best coffee in town.

Her: Really?

You: Why don't you come find out?

If she doesn't drink coffee, you can tell her you make a mean glass of water, Coke, or whatever else you might have. But if you are going to set up this scenario, you should actually have coffee at your house—and clean mugs. Being a bit of a coffee snob, I would be offended if you pulled out Folgers or something instant. Buy good coffee and have cream and sugar on hand. Start thinking of food as sensual.

If things are going really well and she starts touching you or moving closer to you on the way home, you could get to your door and say something like, "I didn't ask you here for the coffee," but you better follow that up with the most earth-shattering kiss you can muster. If she stays on her side of the vehicle, she is probably thinking of all the reasons she shouldn't be doing this, so you will need to continue to be sexy and charming. You should have good music playing in your truck—nothing that will put her to sleep and no Marvin Gaye. Rock music can lend a dangerous feel and keep her awake, but no screamo either.

Music I recommend for the evening is:

- Anything by 30 Seconds to Mars
- Awesome 80s rock like Bon Jovi or Springsteen*
- The Used.

---

*He isn't really 80s, I know.

If she still needs you to ease her fears when you get there, open her door and put your hand on the small of her back once she is out of the car. Have her come into the kitchen with you to make the coffee, and then offer her cream and sugar. If she is shy, she will probably just compliment you on the coffee. If she isn't, she might tell you that it is in fact not the best cup she has ever had. Let her ask you questions and get comfortable and let the conversation flow naturally. Maybe you aren't the best conversationalist. That's okay too.

There is an easy way to remedy this: let her do the talking. Anytime she asks you a question, she is secretly hoping you will ask her the same thing back. So answer her and say, "What about you?" Once you finish the coffee, get close to her, take the mug out of her hands, and kiss her like you mean it.

This kiss should lead you into the bedroom or onto the nearest surface. Please be prepared with more than one condom. She won't be carrying them, and you should be the responsible one.

If she is adventurous, enjoy. If not, look into her eyes in the missionary position so she will feel like she hasn't made a mistake. When you are finished, spoon with her naked or offer to take a shower with her. Wash her hair for her and give her a clean towel.

Kiss her again and make her feel like you like her, but don't give her your number unless you plan on dating her and giving up one-night stands. Take her

number instead. Let her lay with you and feel comfortable for a while if you didn't take a shower, and then offer to take her home because you have to work early, or you're going to a family thing out of town in the morning.

Open her car door for her again and drive her home. When you get to her house, kiss her again like she is the sexiest woman alive and then say goodnight. Don't walk her to her door unless you are planning on seeing her again.

Once she gets out, though, wait in the driveway until you see she gets in safely. It will let her know you aren't a jerk. Then pat yourself on the back all the way home.

Made in the USA
Charleston, SC
06 January 2014